BEYOND MODERNITY

BEYOND MODERNITY

Reflections of a Post-Modern Catholic

by
GEORGE WILLIAM RUTLER

IGNATIUS PRESS   SAN FRANCISCO

Cover by Marcia Ryan

© 1987 Ignatius Press, San Francisco
All rights reserved
ISBN 0–89870–135–x
Library of Congress Catalogue Number 86–82636
Printed in the United States of America

TABLE OF CONTENTS

ACKNOWLEDGMENTS

Some of the material in this book is based on lectures delivered to groups at Sarah Lawrence College, Columbia University, Princeton University, and the Catholic University of America. Several essays originally were published in separate form. The author and Ignatius Press express their gratitude, for permission to reprint these materials in the present book, to the following: *Policy Review,* the *Human Life Review, Catholicism in Crisis,* the *New Oxford Review,* the *Homiletic and Pastoral Review,* the Manresa Educational Corporation, the Cardinal Mindszenty Foundation, the Institute on Religious Life, and the Fellowship of Catholic Scholars. Statements by the President of the Johns Hopkins University in Chapter V are copyright 1985/86 by The New York Times Company. Reprinted by permission. *Modern Times,* copyright 1983 by Paul Johnson, is quoted with permission of Harper and Row Publishers, Inc.

The author also wishes to express his indebtedness to the Reverend Daniel C. Fives, S.S., and Monsignor Florence D. Cohalan.

I

BEYOND MODERNITY:
FACING THE TWENTY–FIRST CENTURY

The modern age is becoming outmoded, the thing it thought most unlikely. This poses a problem overwhelming to set minds: what happens when the age which was supposed to be the end of all the ages ends itself? The stark reply is, modern man is the least equipped to know. While posturing as the breath of things to come, he was instituting the first civilized denial of the future. Modernity is worse than a rejection of the past; it is a defiant avoidance of that which is next, probably the first school of discourse to cancel tomorrow as a thing as vapid as part of yesterday.

It is ungrateful to forget your last breath; it is suffocating to forget your next breath. And it is oppressively tedious. That is not an incidental problem: the modern age has established boredom as its typical form of death. In the process of setting astonishing records in science, as if life were becoming a succession of World's Fairs with confident Cities of the Future on display, modern life became a kind of record stuck in time. The prophet's solemn announcement, "Now is the hour", got worn down, so that his pale adverb had to do the work of his ruddy noun: "Now is". Since the line had nowhere to go, it kept repeating itself. The prophecy became so redundant that the prophets began to call themselves mere existentialists.

Creation has a future; chance does not. The real futurists have been the archivists and evangelists who knew the difference between habits and plans, drawing with rabbinic sagacity a line between movements and progressions. The moderns, having abandoned the sense of Genesis, also lost the heart of the Apocalypse. The end of time became a thought too dreadful to think, something that might at most be intimated by the disappearance of thin snail darters and the appearance of pregnant mushroom clouds. One antidote illusion remained: that the twentieth century was not only the criterion of time, but was time altogether. If history were a scrap heap, the future would be a useless procrastination.

In that rarefied atmosphere, people thought there was something significant, even revolutionary, in the expression, "I am me." Other ages, and one hopes they include the one to come, would say that such a statement is to philosophy what it is to grammar. But the twentieth century did manage to convince itself that it was something more riveting than a fulcrum, for it had no other references to balance or move; and it was even more than a zenith, for it had no legacy of a foundation. It was the very pinpoint of experience. Or so it seemed, for it had confused human essence and human existence. In its isolation from the human tradition, the modern mentality forgot this sharp and central fact: the essential human has his existence from God. The "I" is a thing received. For while each person is a unique entity, a "first subject of attribution", each person is nonetheless subject to God by the fact of creation. If the created "I" does not also morally subject itself by an act of its free will to the Wholly Other who is the only "I Am", then it endures the servility of a false existence. When the modern determinist declares, "I am me", as though that sufficiently defied all that inhibits him, he is merely revealing frustration at not being the "I Am." Without recourse to the unutterable name of God, man cannot even declare himself. Hence humans, who alone of all creatures are capable of an identity crisis, have in their modernity made the crisis a neurosis instead of a moment of revelation. The human mind that does not resolve itself, endlessly afflicts itself.

The affliction takes the form of thinking that your own age is the pinpoint of all viable circumstance and all verifiable truth. The problem for such a mind is this: angels can dance on a pinpoint but people cannot. What must be an exhilarating and expansive dance for pure intelligence (which is what angels are) must be a depressing and confining thing for intelligence obliged to reason (which is what humans are). The mediaeval schoolmen had figured this out, but from around the time of Comte and the modernist rumblings, people rather muddled it. In a symbolic sense, modern man was certain that no angels could dance for lack of legs, but that every human was engaged in dance because he was engaged in having legs. But as the modern dance did not seem very like what angels were supposed to do, modern man decided, as though by some common and unspoken intuition bending and abstracting his art and discourse, that all dances are meant to be sad and limited. The idea was as outdated as a pagan myth, for the pagans had already called such a dance a "tragedy" and had described it with violent and terrible beauty. The notion of the defeated dance has set the mood of outmoded moderns who are by now the most contradictory of philosophical derelicts.

To admit that human creatures are "a little lower than the angels" is prelude to knowing that they are "crowned with glory and honor". Uncomfortable on the head of a pin, the essential man now is trying to assess his rightful place. He is possibly beginning to stretch his logic instead of his ego. At least he is beginning to accept that such a thing can happen; and that such a thing might even be good. He may even be awakening like a wrinkled giant from the hoary modern slumber which dreamed such odd illusions of cause and effect. In fitful modern nights, the most compulsive superstition seemed

convincing; for it actually looked as though supernatural realities,
such as the motivations behind the creation of the universe
itself, have only natural causes; and that natural realities, such
as human responsibility, have supernatural causes in the determinism of economic and psychological compulsions. In separating from God, the modern impulse became detached from
itself: in theology the illusion came to be "modernism". But
the term "modernity" refers to the whole condition of alienated culture. It bespoke an ineffable melancholy in the midst of
a magisterial Darwinism, more ready than human curiosity
ever was to examine its origins and more uncertain than ever
about its purpose. Matthew Arnold's vast chagrin at the "long,
withdrawing roar" of the Sea of Faith, drifted from Dover
Beach until it became the plaintive voice of the existentialist
refused by the sea itself on every beach.

I hope the prospect of an awakening from this fractious
sleep is not unduly optimistic. Optimism is an obscured will's
substitute for hope. I hope then that the prospect of a twenty-
first century more aware of spiritual order is not unfounded.
Of this we can be certain, shocking as it may be: modern
assumptions are lending themselves to the past tense, and the
boast "now is" has started to sound like "then was".

For one thing, modern students no longer rush to the barri-
cades for modernity because they have become professors barri-
cading themselves against the students. The rebelliousness of
the new young is in their refusal to rebel. The one spark of
defiance, other than a general conservatism, is a lassitude and a
sensuality mocking well the satiety of the senior generation.
This is immensely irritating to the greying moderns who had
expected the modern age to have become permanent by now.
But that expectation itself was the very asp which modernity
pressed against its own bosom. It let loose a notion of permanent instability, of horizontal revolution, of eternal transience,

of ancient youth under the panoply of a godless religion and a sacred state; and each of its adjectives bit and poisoned each of its nouns. Modernity stood for irreverence and ended bowing before it; it respected no age older than youth and aged doing it. That swirling mixture of energy, pettiness, valor, narrow-mindedness, inventiveness, softness, cruelty, impatience, excitement, boredom, pragmatism, and escapism called modernity is freezing in the face of a fact more petrifying than Medusa. It can be uttered in barely more than a coarse whisper; it dare not be gazed at by more than a wink. It is this: the only modern people left are old people.

Politics and Religion

In the present circumstance, it has become difficult to discuss anything having to do with politics which with sharp pertinence does not have to do with theology. Secular newspapers and magazines give surprising coverage to the social implications of dogmatic issues. The facts are a lesson in how the modern mind misjudged itself. Many intellectuals at the beginning of the twentieth century took for granted that, by now, mention of God would be relegated to advertisements placed in the back pages by residual fideists. This has not happened. The current quality of commentary is generally low, but it is to a certain extent the fruit of a sincere attempt to assess the durability of the idea of God.

Deep themes like abortion and euthanasia appear in daily political debate for a substantial reason, and not for the sake of contentiousness alone. Human achievements, doubts, suppositions, and experiments have to find their resolution in the definition of life, where all ultimate resolutions repose. Vital activities can be categorized, but they cannot be isolated in a culture. The greatness of human acts requires that they be formed according to those basic values which have unified the varieties of experience in each authentic social enterprise. The essentials are those capacities known by the civilized as "rights"; without them, men and women would be forced to exist as creatures without souls.

The Pursuit of Happiness

By an intuition common to thinkers who have not divorced themselves from reality, America's political architects drew great draughts from the scheme of natural law as the scholastics had laid it out in order: life, then liberty, and then pursuit of happiness. Happiness is posited in the Catholic moral tradition as the final purpose of human life, and all rights are geared toward its attainment. Human acts, to be human, have to aim for that complete happiness which is called blessedness, or the supernatural joy which is happiness in the possession of one's good.

There is no potential for happiness without liberty; and you need life to have liberty. There are many offenses against the dignity of life because the modern age has thrown off reasonable discourse in the breathless chase down quick paths to contentment. The hunt has bogged down in a Dionysian hollow where it does not even seem possible to define existence. This just bears out the axiom: without the patient sanity of the muses, happiness becomes little more than amusement. Pope John Paul II told Canadian teenagers: "Have the courage to resist the dealers in deception who make capital of your hunger for happiness and who make you pay dearly for a moment of 'artificial paradise', a whiff of smoke, a bout of drinking, or drugs. What claims to be a shortcut to happiness leads nowhere."

The senescent can skip down that primrose path as gingerly as the adolescent. The modern anxiety comes from seeking sensible consolations apart from insensible graces; it is a problem basically because consolation has been confused with grace.

The virtuous hunger for happiness is located in the soul, as it is the composite of intellect and will. The intellect discerns good and bad, and the will chooses between them. These endowments separate humans from other living things and make us "in the image of God". When the intellect and will are compromised by philosophies of "nonsense" and "aimlessness", the perception of happiness diminishes, and the world as a mirror of aspiration becomes ever cloudier, as Saint Paul taught in his first letter to the Corinthians.

Of course modern man does not deny the primacy of happiness as his primary end. He speaks of it almost obsessively in terms of fulfillment. Every normal person desires it, and thinks that it is at least theoretically attainable, even if not satisfactorily capable of definition: at work, at home, in each romance. But the secular confinements of the imagination dull a basic point here, and the blunting happens so subtly that one may not notice it at first. It is something like not seeing that a wall needs repainting until some picture frame is removed to reveal the original color beneath. The original truth overlooked is the blatant principle: in order to be fulfilled (that is, in order to be filled full), you have to be capable of being filled; and to be capable of being filled, you have to be capable of being. When all the world had been stained by pride, there was a moment like a light and breath out of time, when a thing shone white as a Christ and a voice as long as an Eternity announced: "I am not come to destroy but to fulfill" (Mt 5:17). Some who heard thought they had come within range of contrariness, when in truth it was the effective contradiction of nonsense.

Like the first mistaken people who stood in the light without knowing it, modern man has thought that the original color of the world was merely an old color. As a result, he has become nearly oblivious to the brightest implications of what it is "to be". God promised fulfillment, but only upon confrontation with the divine identity as "I Am." Rejecting that, modern being tried to pass through the multiple corridors of the twentieth century as an autonomous utterance, with neither subject nor object for its action, fated as those who "measure themselves by one another, and compare themselves with one another" (2 Cor 10:12). Not surprisingly then, the articulation of this journey has become more or less a series of grunts. The modern consciousness may find itself juxtaposed between pessimistic and providential expectations, and wonder where in fact it is. But its wonder has become less wonderful and more quizzical, and that because it has lost its spiritual motivation.

This motivation, or sense of plan, is more precisely a "memory". Any progress requires a memory; navigation is proof of a reference. Memory gives measure. When an Englishwoman was first shown the Pacific and told that it was larger than the Atlantic, she obligingly replied, "So I see." Her situation is not without analogy. Deprived of authentic memory, one can measure only by the visible, which must mean being bound by the horizon.

The latest intelligence knows that the world is not flat, as did many reasonable ancients. But there were some primitives who did think the world flat, not because they knew it to be flat but because they felt it to be so. This was a sentimentalism alien to classical thinkers but typical of modernity. Sentimentalism is a wild saboteur in the halls of logic, and it has committed deep defacements in the twentieth century. There are modern existentialists so deprived of rational reference that they have become oppressed by horizontality; they cannot help fantasizing that the soul is flat. Even the primitive flatlanders were rarely so crude as to be flatsoulers. But there are moderns who have become so; and when they are told about human creatures who are well-rounded, or "holy", they shake their heads saying such poor people must have gone off the deep end. The secret of holiness is the deepest enigma for modern consciousness: the desire for perfection is the sane evidence that humans have a high purpose in an eternal plan. But the desire for self-perfection is insane, even as the horizontal existentialist tries to make it replace holiness; St. Augustine exposed it long before the modern madness rolled in: "I am caught up to Thee by Thy love, only to be swept back by my own weight" (*Confessions* 7:17).

The Present Trauma

Intelligence recollects the most important events with the help of theology, that critical faculty of the mind which shapes the well-roundedness of the human spirit by considering the perfection of God. A progressive analysis of a historical and psychological kind is going to be theological if it is to reflect on truth and not become the reflection of bias. The modern age, and this has been repeated *ad nauseam* though not often enough *ad theologiam,* has been a time of the most rapid changes fostered by a brilliance and forced by a brutishness. Men and women who used horse and carriage have seen a human gallop on the face of the moon. Engineering, genetics, migrations, the rapid communication of news and ideas, have affected and almost overwhelmed billions on every continent. With so much news, it is not easy to tolerate anything that is not new. This has consequences for the ability to trust existence, since being is the oldest thing

beings have done. Paul Johnson has given an account in his
Modern Times:

> The old order had gone . . . there were disquieting currents of
> thought which suggested the image of a world adrift, having
> left its moorings in traditional law and morality. There was too
> a new hesitancy on the part of the established and legitimate
> authority to get the global vessel back under control by the
> accustomed means, or any means. . . . Of the great trio of Ger-
> man imaginative scholars who offered explanations of human
> behavior in the nineteenth century and whose corpus of thought
> the post-1918 world inherited . . . Marx described a world in
> which the central dynamic was economic interest. To Freud, the
> principal thrust was sexual. Both assumed that religion, the
> old impulse which moved men and masses, was a fantasy. . . .
> Nietzsche was also an atheist. He saw God not as an invention
> but a casualty, and his demise . . . an historical event, which
> would have dramatic consequences. He wrote in 1886: "The
> greatest event of recent times—that God is Dead, that the belief
> in the Christian God is no longer tenable—is beginning to cast
> its first shadows over Europe." Among the advanced races, the
> decline and ultimately the collapse of the religious impulse
> would leave a large vacuum. The history of modern times is in
> great part the history of how that vacuum has been filled. . . . In
> place of religious belief, there would be secular ideology.

Pope John XXIII discerned the inheritance of a whirlwind
attendant upon that vacuum, and called his cardinals together
at the basilica of St. Paul-outside-the-Walls to announce a
universal council of the Church. It was the middle of the
twentieth century; and the Church, with her antecedents and
directions, now had to guard and teach this more effectively in
the trauma of change: "man" and "twentieth century man" are
not an adequate equation. The Second Vatican Council would
say:

Ours is a new age of history with critical and swift upheavals spreading gradually to all corners of the earth. They are the products of man's intelligence and creative activity, but they recoil upon him, upon his judgments and desires, both individual and collective, upon his ways of thinking and acting in regard to people and things.... In probing the recesses of his own mind, man often seems more uncertain than ever of himself: in the gradual and precise unfolding of the laws of social living, he is perplexed by uncertainty about how to plot its course.... A transformation of this kind brings with it the serious problems associated with any crisis of growth ... (*Gaudium et Spes,* 4.2).

The Analysis of Growth

There are two kinds of growth: the first we do, the second we have. One is the necessary kind of transformation—physical, intellectual, spiritual, without which we decline and die. The other is a malignant distortion. Growth makes me live. A growth makes me die. "Be not conformed to this world: but be transformed by the renewing of your mind, that you may discern what is the good, acceptable and perfect will of God" (Rom 12:2). This is the foundation of being: transformation of the creature according to the purposes of the Creator. God is the reference for the tension between the varieties of growth, and the trail of the growth itself is the inclusive subject of history.

Humans are living creatures because they are chronological creatures. They live because they have pasts and futures. They inhale and exhale, and every breath becomes a testament to history. They do not merely live by one breath, and they do not dwell in one capsule of time. Obvious as this may seem, almost to the point of a truism, it flies in the face of contemporary sentiment. Modernity's lack of tradition has made modern life a kind of moral mutation.

"Modern" means "precisely now" according to its Latin root; but with equivalent Latinity it can mean "only now" and this is the difficulty. If modern man lives "for the moment", he loses his capacity for the moment past, the hour ago, the year before; he has little inclination to lift his eyes toward an approaching scene. With the rapidity of events, and the almost simultaneous report of them, there is hardly time to synthesize them without appearing to produce something inadequate.

To live for the moment is to be cut off from the beginning, from the end, from the whole continuum; and thus it is essentially to be perplexed by, and even alienated from, the immediate moment too. God gave man "dominion" according to the witness of Genesis, and this includes, by interpretation, the ability to master the content of historical experience. The alternative is to be victimized by it, enslaved rather than transformed through grace by circumstance, the world, and the flesh. The spiritual consequence then is sinfulness and the cultural result is trendiness. Human control erodes to an inability even to express what is going on. People begin to account for the human pageant with expressions like: "It's what's happening", and "Like it's now", and "Right on", and "He's where it's at", and "I hear where you're coming from", and even "Like I mean, you know, you don't know how to communicate." Words are universals; inability to speak them coherently marks the loss of a comprehensive perception of natural order.

Consider some of the individuals walking along the streets of New York City listening to radios or actually wearing earphones, wrapped in an audient incubus, breathing embodiments of the solipsism and psychological atomism the philosophers wrote about. And there is the more dismal representation of divorce from temporal reality as it is accounted in the divorce of husbands from wives, marriage being the most intimate form of social history. These separations may be veiled, the isolations inhabited, but no engineer or lethal doctor can annul the fact of disorder.

The Sacred Scriptures begin "In the beginning" and end with the shout "Maranatha" (Come, Lord). The beginning of God's word is the end of ignorance and the end of God's word is the beginning of everything else. To be bound to only an interval of that is to be crippled by trends and not freed by tradition. In the context of salvation history, tradition passes the art of transformation from one generation to the next. Any captivity to the incidental moment is perceptibly hurtful. The trendy adult feels the sting when newly-arrived youths call him old-fashioned and treat his epoch as a vignette.

Modern Landmarks

Prodigies of modern physical science well antedate the twentieth century; one looks back to the mid-nineteenth century and Maxwell's study of the magnetic field, the use of the X-ray, the discovery of the radioactivity of uranium, and Rutherford's definition of the structure of the atom. But Spencer's kind of pseudo-science, or scientism, needed something with much more dramatic philosophical implications to break with objectivity, and it was provided in 1905 by Einstein's postulation of his theory of the general relativity of matter. When Einstein was corroborated by solar photographs in 1919, the tremor of relativity became an earthquake in popular philosophy. The theory in fact gave a cosmological boost to the concept of sacred eternity instead of modern commitment to an infinite universe; but scientism had its way once again at the expense of facts.

In 1901 Planck had introduced the quantum theory which Bohr applied to atomic structure in 1912. The more or less static Newtonian idea of passive particles ended, calling into popular doubt any confidence in stable structures except on the macroscopic level of perception. Bohr went to the length of rejecting the concept of cosmos; any questions of ontology and causality were, literally, out of the question. In 1927, Heisenberg's principle of indeterminism in the measurement of conjugate variables furthered the impression of a universe far more unconformable and less linear than the Euclidean could have imagined in his most bewildered reverie. The indeterminacy principle really had nothing to do with elementary particles; but the human inhabitant of his kind planet, already assaulted by the whole cosmos without, felt a sharper stab from every atom within his constitutive world. There were those who began to think that if statues were in fact floating, every hero and heroism itself were unstable and ephemeral notions. Having realized the ageless desire to fly through the sky, the modern man might have felt sadder than Icarus as he seemed to drift through curved time in a world not only round but wavy.

Geniuses are one thing; their disciples are another, sometimes lagging behind and "murmuring in their hearts". Some students of the masters began to apply a physical law to the moral order. Even some of the masters, like Bohr, encouraged them by assuming that the problems of inexact measure, in the world of quanta and waves, meant that knowledge itself is ultimately subjective. Once it was understood that there is a state of relativity in the nature of things, even though nothing could have been more absolute than Einstein's own position on measuring the speed of light, it was popularly supposed that there might be a relativity about truth in the moral and spiritual economies.

It was a surrealistic equation drawn illegitimately from realistic formulas; general relativity and quantum are realist perceptions, and Einstein insisted that creation science must require belief in the objective reality of the universe. The essay which completed his exposition of general relativity in 1917 was directed at the cosmological implications of the theory. It is not far-fetched to see in the Einstein of these lines the modern equivalent in physics of Dr. Johnson kicking a rock to refute the philosophical immaterialism of Bishop Berkeley. As Stanley Jaki has shown in various writings, Einstein was the successor to only two other basically indefective cosmologists. In the eighteenth century Lambert had postulated a centric, hierarchic, and finite universe; in the nineteenth century, Zöllner described a finite mass which generates a closed space of four dimensions. Einstein then provided what the others had not: a fully developed case for specificity, and in doing so he devastated the "infinity catastrophe", or gravitational paradox, by which atheists theoretically maintained an uncreated universe. An agnostic, Einstein realized the implications of his ordered and coherent cosmos and thought it necessary to assure his friends that he had "not yet fallen into the hands of priests".

But as observers are coming to appreciate at this late hour with a vast moral wreckage around them, when relativity fell into the hands of ideological atheists, it simply became confused with relativism; it was parallel to the formation of scientism out of science, as Spencer and Huxley had tried to apply physical science to metaphysical facts outside their competence. These fatal confusions have ushered in a panoply of material doubts, with attendant effects on philosophy and psychology, not to mention religion. Einstein wrote to Solovine in a famous letter of 1952: "What priests will do with my cosmology cannot be helped. Let the devil take care of that." And it would seem that the devil did take jealous care: instead of priests

incorporating realist cosmology in a natural theology, many of
them have widely been intimidated into insecure subjectivity
and sentimentalism by shabby philosophical caricatures of the
new science.

In 1910, Pavlov had already outlined a new hieroglyph of
man as the servant of conditioned reflexes; the picture was filled
in when Watson articulated the science of behaviorism in 1914.
Schools of phenomenology and existentialism commandeered
the philosophical terrain; and Heidegger, Marcel, and Jaspers
struggled in variously tortuous ways with what came to be
known as the "problem" of being. And like Jacob wrestling
with the angel, those who tackled the brooding problem were
put out of joint. Freud and Husserl sought rational explana-
tions for the irrational estimation of the self, but even Freud
came to realize the futility of that. It was left to the National
Socialists to ritualize irrationalism through the dark channels
of Teutonic myth. Incoherent subjectivism leads inevitably to
social tyranny. The analysis of Viktor Frankl, called the third
school of Viennese psychiatry, was a creditable attempt to
trace the mass of psychic disorders to a loss of the sense of
value; he had detected the modern pathology, although his
innocence of metaphysics would keep him part of it to some
degree. At the age of eighty, Frankl repeats with dignity his
old observation of the crisis: "You're always forced, ordered,
to feel joy, to be happy and experience pleasure. This is precisely what obviates the possibility of enjoying oneself."

Surviving in a world whose very idea of harmony caused
discord among subjectivists, the arts took on an attitude contradictory to art. Fine art became something of a refined cramp.
In *fin de siecle* Vienna, which Karl Kraus would call "the testing
lab for the end of the world", Gustav Klimt seceded from his
own aesthetic Secessionist movement. Adolf Loos published a
minimalist summons, "Decoration as Crime". Classical allusion

vanished in Picasso's "Les Demoiselles d'Avignon" of 1907. Kandinsky's first abstract painting in 1910 initiated the primacy of form, and not felicity of form, as an end in itself. In the Zurich of 1917, Dadaism took its name from the language of the cradle, and by some sort of aesthetic sleight of hand, artists who had been the steady nurses of culture shifted to the place of those who are nursed.

Reductionism as tyranny is evident even now in architecture. In 1907 the first "modern" factory was constructed in Berlin; in 1911 the first "modern" house appeared in Vienna. The 1907 *Deutsches Werkbuch* laid out utility as beauty. Aristotle had possibly been the first to say it; but one need only look about at the monochromatic steel and glass boxes anesthetizing the urban environment to see what happens when a good slogan is juggled until it means that utility is the single beauty. Then it becomes a pathetic sight, a dormant aspiration, a Sleeping Beauty as chilling as the hibernation of the whole human kingdom. And if anyone were to utter a protest, or to say that some older things were lovelier than the new, he would be dismissed as puerile and retrograde. In such slumber, minimalist sculptors like Dubuffet and Nevelson, and others whose effusions have hardened in the various metropolitan plazas, claimed that a higher vision is irrelevant: art is self-expression. The obsessions reached a nadir at the Museum of Modern Art in New York, in 1960, as Jean Tinguely exhibited a machine designed to blow itself up. When it did, the people applauded. Everything that we might have to say by way of comment from here on, is probably best heard in the echo of that applause.

Schopenhauer, a natural subjectivist in spite of his rejection of all proofs of divine existence, had called architecture the least ethereal of the servile arts in contrast to the liberal arts of music, arithmetic, and logic; modern architecture had the chance to refute that by placing its tremendous technological advances in the service of delight and creative elegance. But the result of the functionalist experiment was to debase plastic arts altogether in a worse servility. It denuded the imagination of its obligation to a transcendent Being "whose service is perfect freedom". Art, to be art, depicts the children of God under the vault of heaven one way or another; failure to do that makes them feel at least like drones, diminished by some vast material imposition rather than ennobled by monumentality. But time has its revenge, and the revenge comes quickly in the modern calculation; commissions have been formed in most civilized places to prevent further destruction of good buildings. Twenty years ago, when sensitivities were lacking, the magnificent Pennsylvania Station in Manhattan was torn down to make room for a new crackerbox Madison Square Garden and station which are already slated for demolition.

When the universe is represented as a sublimation of the minimalizing ego, dominion becomes willfulness, and the imagination becomes intent upon dehumanizing acts and ugly constructions. The Anti-Artist takes over, and the belligerent Satan shrieks to the God of rainbows and golden speech: *"Non serviam!"*—I will not serve.

Music got caught in the rebellion; what Mahler spoke of as melodic *angstneurose* began to hurt even human song. Almost without noticing it themselves, people have stopped gathering around the family piano to sing. In part, it is a domestic price paid for what now is known as Schönberg's atonalism, or what he called pantonalism in the masterly *Harmonielehre* of 1911: a concept so cerebral that it almost seems too delicate to blame for clubbing to death all the jolly sing-alongs. But its fingerprints are there. It first appeared almost innocuously in the finale of his Second String Quartet in 1907, a whimper from the strange and darkened passageway of souls and nations drawing closer to theoretical combat: Adrian Leverkühn, the demon musician in Thomas Mann's *Dr. Faustus,* is Nietzsche and Schönburg wrapped in one. In a line quite horrible for what it portends, Maurice Blanchot said Schönburg had freed thought from "the tyranny of unity". Years later, at the other end of the line of misadventure, The Beatles produced a song not for any sunny home and hearth: "Nowhere Man". Between the Mozartian composer as the "mouthpiece of God" and the latest acid rock stars with their attendant dark symbols, the difference is ominously patent. Even old war chants had a terrible dignity about them; the new trend of stark hate songs imposes a more terrible degradation. And any pursuit of relief in the banality of television fare as home entertainment is an assault on integrity less only by pedantic degree.

In the books lying on modernity's shelves, Camus, Ionesco, and Beckett used different kinds of diction to expose man as the "useless passion" Sartre called him to his face. Books demand better attention than a glimpse; but the devolution of literature has produced a backward genre in which the content becomes more shallow the more it is fathomed. And something else is quite as wrong: the remaining writers of stout heart who courageously deny the futility of life too often pluck small subjects and miniature themes to prove their point, as though altruism could supplant transcendence.

Why has modern man wound up looking at himself as a spectacle he cannot join? The rhetorical question deserves at least a rhetorical answer. Plainly, he thinks he has come of age when in fact he is suffering from a clinical case of arrested development. He appears to have decided, in the glare of its shining and wonderful works, that the twentieth century is the definitive and culminative age, a kind of litmus of all life and the ages. And though some of this century's glare has been from cities and populations on fire, he has concluded that the moral evolution is complete:

that it needs only the guidance of spontaneous goodness and benevolent programs sponsored by governments and institutions larger than himself. We know the name for this, for it has been tossed about in ways both good and glib: it is secular humanism which, upon analysis, has been neither very worldly nor humane.

Ashes scattered by relativism and determinism, in the name of secularity, cannot properly be called new structures. Hitler and Stalin and Mao took the flight from the vital humane tradition to extremes, lighting up ghastly wars along the way, leaving chivalrous belligerents exhausted and sceptical. After the Second World War, in the glow of its finest hour, with little protest, the free West slid into its present slough of sensuality and moral indifference. The new mode was so easily adapted, that to criticize it is to provoke an instantaneous reaction of bemusement and curiosity. As situation ethics filled the void which had been left from the demise of rational and objective discourse, the modern thinker tried the best he could to confront malaise; but he could not convincingly overcome his fear of death, the ultimate absurdity. Instead of old voices asking, "Who are you?", crisp new voices only ask, "What do you do?" and "How much do you make?" As for the old question, the modern mind has been left to mull it over on his own; but to answer it would be to talk to himself. The prophets of wisdom and the bells of inspiration are few. With a casual pathos, the modern man yields to the whole cacophony in that telling moment when he meets a friend and offers to buy him a drink in the same kind tones with which he used to offer to give him one.

Beyond This

That there should be a pervasive sense of dissatisfaction, of unease, of a loneliness called alienation from the very creation humans were meant to master, is a halting sign of promise: like a bad pulse instead of none at all. The sense of a moral abyss, no matter how intimidating, is a faint gesture of surrender to reality. And the most discerning reality that comes to us is the knowledge that we have been created by God; and not only by him, but positively for him. Precocious Augustine abandoned his private version of modernity in the year 386 when his eyes fell on the sacred words: "Let us behave decently, as in the daytime . . ." (Rom 13:13). Later, he added words of his own: "You did make us, Lord, for your own; and our hearts are restless until they find their rest in You."

Everyone can add words. For instance, one might say that man did indeed come of age in the twentieth century; and then we would be saddled with the corollary which means that twenty-first-century man will be senile. Or one might say that history is still going on even as sophisticates mock it and pedants ignore it. The amnesia of modern man is cured by the eucharistic "anamnesis", or "un-forgetting", of man eternal. This is deeper than remembering an event; it is the entrance to that which gives coherence to all events. But this requires a movement past the old theological and philosophical afflictions of many centuries: the Reformation idea of an irredeemably corrupt human nature, and the imperious cynicism of Machiavelli and his successors, denied the eucharistic soul access to the grand sacramental scene; it is incontestable that they prepared the way for petty consumerism, existentialism, and even surrealism. As T. S. Eliot symbolizes in his pilgrimage from J. Alfred Prufrock to Thomas à Becket, anything valuable of post-modern life will be that which was valuable in pre-modern life; at the heart of all human value since the first Day of Resurrection is the Eucharist of Catholicism.

The New Re-Ordering

The essential eucharistic vision is being aided now by a vast cosmology whose erudition puts the monopoly of sensate empiricism on the defensive. The most recent discoveries, of which the 3°K cosmic background radiation of the "Big Bang" is emblematic, are making the Biblical account of creation *ex nihilo* not only plausible, but palpable, to the physicist. Given the vividness of singularities which cosmologists now discern in the space-time structure of the universe, it will be up to the post-modern cosmologist to reject the philosophical revulsion of modernity toward the principle of causality. Having inherited the subjectivist bias through Locke, Hume, and Kant, modern science rejected the possibility of a coherent reality independent of human impression. The arbitrariness was not true science, we may now dare to say; it was the scientism of which we have spoken, the same sort of prejudice which led to the condemnation of cosmology in the Soviet Union in the late 1930s as "bourgeois metaphysics".

The ground of authentic scientific research is Judaeo-Christian realism: that is, the proper taming of limited idealism and empiricism by the analytically confident mind which comprehends the contingent cosmos because it is a reflection of the non-contingent mind of God. This line is about to be lifted from modernity's scrap heap of incongruous literature, to be given a portent we can hardly imagine right now: "So God created man in his own image, in the image of God he created him; male and female he created them ... " (Gen 1:27).

Though it is too early for the experts to estimate the significance of the discovery of residual radiation for the developing schools of creation theory, the precise recording of evidence for the Big Bang by Wilson and Penzias already a quarter of a century ago may come to be regarded as the crucial intimation

of post-modernity, something like the way Einstein's model of
general relativity made modernity self-conscious. The implications of an act of creation were seen as a threat to modernity
fifty years ago when Nernst, the Nobel laureate physicist,
refused to calculate without infinity and continued to ignore
the evidence of radioactivity. Though not theologians, the
astrophysicists Sir Fred Hoyle and Chandra Wickramasinghe
already represent what we might presume to call the post-
modern rejection of Nernst's scientism; they actually allow a
place for teleology, or the study of purpose, in cosmology.
Modernity rejected the possibility of non contingent Being,
and thus faltered in its analysis of contingency. Recovery from
that could lead human thought to a new integrity and scope
for science in which theology, cosmology, and anthropology
will amplify the harmony in the Biblical psalms of creation.
The university could become a university again, and the physicist might approach the Eucharist with the reverence of the
metaphysicist. In an address to the Philadelphia Society in
1980, Stanley Jaki spoke as a priest and physicist:

> . . . special and general relativity make sense only if there is an
> orderly and coherent totality of things, a universe which declares
> by its very specificity, say by the value of its space-time curva-
> ture and the size of its total mass, that it is a contingent being.
> Such a universe provides one half of that arch which is the
> cosmic connection between science and religion. The other half
> of that arch is that and only that religion which, *first,* has a
> dogma in the words, I believe in God, the Father Almighty,
> Maker of Heaven and Earth, of all things visible and invisible,
> and *second,* does not dilute that Almighty Father into a mere
> incident of process theology, and *third,* does not deny that the
> content of that dogma is accessible to reason.

In the last moment of serious modernity, the Beat Generation denied the credal and eucharistic reality of man by mak-

ing cynicism lyrical. Physics was as irrelevant to the *jongleurs* of isolation as metaphysics had been. They were succeeded soon enough by the Hippies who attempted some kind of return to primeval innocence through the self-absorbing fogs of a fabricated Aquarian age. But the soul cannot "return to the soil" by breaking up the concrete that has been poured over it; and no one can "go back to nature" by offering the unnatural Prince of Lies a garland of flowers. The deflowering of the Flower Children ceded place to the new generation of Young Urban Professionals, counterparts of Desdemona's suitors in *Othello,* the "wealthy curled darlings", the vulgar victims of indulgence. They may be no less self-conscious or cosmically ignorant, and no less rapacious; but they do give some evidence of willingness to consider a wisdom deeper than a fad, with a past and a prologue to their own moment. If they can repair their defective educations and isolation from their own souls, they may yet avoid sinking silently into their pretentious and bottomless utopias.

There are signs of a readjustment of sensibilities in unlikely places. In certain classrooms, free verse is yielding to rhyme schemes; and there are reports in some cities of instruction in "touch dancing". Leonard Bernstein's Norton Lectures on tonality are taken more seriously now than they were in 1973. Having dismantled even vernacular literacy, certain school systems are beginning to teach history as history and not as sociology, and are turning to classical languages for help. These instances still are rare, and may have little impact without a commensurate recovery of family life to support the new interest in substance; but they mark a trend not predicted a generation ago. Robert Stern, Michael Graves, Robert Venturi, Thomas Gordon Smith, and other architects who deliberately call themselves post-modern, are puzzling an older generation of modern architects by saying: if form follows function, it is all the more vital that function be graced by a loveliness of form. Applied decoration, which the International Style placed under interdict, is liberated. The beauty of patterns is not cosmetic, and the tradition of order is not a masquerade.

In religion, the new interest in classical sources is so pervasive that even clergymen cannot stop it. There was a time when books were written by modern Catholics looking at their outdated Church; now the Church perennial is looking at outdated modern Catholics. Dissenters from immutable doctrine are quite more old guard than avant-gard, as they keep custody of an outlook long since proved unworkable, typically Kantian epistemologists who have been trapped while fleeing the implications of a realist metaphysics. And in the manner of those who hold the common man in contempt, they are the most bourgeois in their suspicion of the deep kind of change which can come about by classicism. Theologians who see Church doctrine as "a weight to be lifted as soon as possible", said Cardinal Ratzinger, are expressing a "middle-class Christianity". For all their talk about free speech they are the most bigoted thought patrols on the campus.

Here is the core of the matter. By trying to create a classless society as the epitome of relativist idealism, modern man came close to making everyone middle-class; and that is why the culture of the West fears the end of the modern age as it did not fear the end of the agrarian age or of the industrial age. The choleric reaction of old-guard modernists actually becomes censorious and abusive, like the fourteen publishers who rejected Orwell's *Animal Farm* for its violation of utopia. The modern age taught us how confining open-mindedness can be; how defensive the progressivist is; how restricting free thought makes itself; how many things are sacrosanct to the scoffer. And when all this is seen at the end of an age, there is a startling thing to be heard. Modern man whimpers, then shrieks, that he has been betrayed. There is no sound shriller than the shattering of an iconoclast.

Prospects

The pre-Socratic philosopher Empedocles pretended to make himself a god by plunging into the crater of Aetna; according to one version, the resident gods mocked his suicide by tossing out one of his sandals. Modern man was Empedocles, and the post-moderns are left now holding his sandal and wondering what to make of the whole vacant scene. If post-modernism were a movement rather than a condition, a crank reaction or romantic repristinization instead of a realization, it should be dismissed by anyone who takes Christianity seriously. Certainly post-modernism, even when schizophrenic about its reasons and purposes, has to be more than historicist revivalism if it is to be anything; no one but a reactionary thinks he can recover from scientism by lapsing into historicism, or defensive archaism. Historicism is a clamp on the significance of history, as scientism puts a clamp of its own on the grandeur of science. If the post-modern conscience looks back, it must be to the ancient and changeless things that give direction to those things that should change. And it must certainly be other than a secular neo-conservatism about politics, for such cannot meet the demands of the questions being asked. The integrity of culture is founded in a metaphysical responsibility. Without that, political rightists and leftists are just alternating versions of the same destructive current.

The appearance of the twenty-first century will be more precise than a trend and much like a tide. The year 2000, after all, is only a symbolic mark for what is now under way, just as the nineteenth-century idealists had launched modern expression before the twentieth century called itself modern. Post-modernity does not even have an adequate name for itself. The term "post-modern" gives a kind of pivotal status to things modern. The modern age may just as well be called pre-post-modern. The time will come for a name, but we will not be the ones to give it. This one definition remains: the essence of modernity was its desire to live without deference or reference to God and with an abiding sense of inexplicable alienation in time and space. Modernity thought that facts were caused by clocks and calendars which in truth can only time them; then it unrealistically denied the future by claiming to have become it. To be post-modern is to syncopate chronology and ontology again, and to reaffirm the fact of God who has "placed before you an open door that no one can shut" (Rev 3:7).

A leader of the 1960s "Death of God" school has died convinced that the Shroud of Turin is authentic. And a theologian who extolled the "Secular City" in 1965 has newly written a book which tries to account for religion as it perdures in that city; this is the same interval of years separating the fall of Rome from the completion of St. Augustine's *City of God.* But there are evidences of a vigor more animated than these. The most compelling voices are those that say what they have long said: life is so important that it is worth giving up a life to secure. More priests fell dead before their altars during the Spanish Civil War than during the persecutions of Nero and Decius. In Vietnam, bishops have been placed under house arrest; between 1981 and 1984, seven Albanian bishops were tortured to death; over the last thirty years, the Christian martyrs of China have been beyond count; nearly ten million Ukrainian Catholics have been annihilated since the First World War in one of the best kept secrets of the century. Stalin ordered more crucifixions than Pilate. And into the heart of the hecatomb new reminders of social honesty keep walking:

nuns in India, labor leaders in Poland, popes travelling to the nations.

Simultaneously, Liberal Protestantism is evaporating as a social presence, and its account of nature and grace makes a weak appeal to the very populations it sought to encourage. Cartesian epistemology has grown sterile in the whirlwind of new phenomenology. Marxist dogmas on matter, super-structures, and the proletariat are crumbling before the latest testimonies of cosmology and history. The resulting vacuum in thought and culture is unprecedented in the chronicles of the West and East. The stunned emptiness, indicated by the depopulation and lethargy of Europe as the cradle of modernity, envelops any inadequate and novel commentary to justify itself; but it may next surrender, like any delicate lacuna, to some consciousness of a Creator who abhors a vacuum more than does his creation, and who condemned the modern fail-ure when he spoke in history's oldest moment: "It is not good for man to be alone" (Gen 2:18b).

At least this can be said: some guardians of culture may be alarmed and even depressed at the post-modern advent; they most likely will be, if they have been diluting their pedagogy and spirituality to make it palatable to modern taste. They cannot reasonably continue to pass off this social transition as some fatuous neo-conservatism, or facile neo-orthodoxy. Neo-conservatism is a laissez-faire form of alienation if it lacks the unifying spiritual tradition; and without sanctity, neo-orthodoxy is a revived obscurantism. Orthodoxy is not enough, not for the evangelization of the post-modern world: orthodoxy is the teaching of truth, and truth is unfulfilled without holiness. The work of reordering society is immensely broad and grave, as well as happy, and its integrity is endowed supernaturally.

The leader of the Catholic world told the bishops of Europe in 1985: "The great evangelizers of Europe have been the saints. We must supplicate the Lord to increase the Church's spirit of holiness and send us new saints to evangelize today's world." So begins the pageant of the re-evangelization of the West. The integrity of intellects and wills too acute for relativism, and too free for determinism, is enlisting many of the generation now rising, for whom the twentieth century's protests of loneliness will be an obscure echo. They will not find the reclamation of truth easy, and to every other obstacle which has been a parcel of the human saga is now added another: modernity habituated itself to rewarding mediocrity and it is a habit hard to break. The institutions of society in every enterprise impose a near obligation to be mediocre. With rare exceptions, the leaders are faceless, the heroes are anti-heroes, the guides shun excellence, and the great are gnawed at by the small. Perils of greatness are not new, but the pervasive social pact with triteness is a novel phenomenon. In such an environment, a new generation may find it difficult to get straight answers. Those that do will find them in the Christian humanism where they have been found without interruption in spite of every attempt to obscure them over the centuries. The youth of the first post-modern generation may not comprehend the answers when they have located them, at least not at first. But, in any circumstance, they will break company with the old moderns who did not comprehend the questions.

II

RELIGION AND THE NEWSPAPERS

Bigotry

Conspicuousness can turn an object of interest into a target. The Roman Catholic Church has been a singularly conspicuous fact of civilization for nearly two thousand years: the broad side of the barn which some may miss but not the narrow side which no one aims at; not a wedge but the thing wedged into by everything else, reformer and vandal alike; the inn of the ages and not the guest of the moment. Journalists write about the Church because it is very large, and that is as good a reason as most; but that also gives some of them an excuse to take liberties, as in vaudeville where most of the pies are thrown at stout people. According to this code, an assault is not an enormity if the object of the attack is enormous. The child abuser is the lowest of types; but that is no reason for making heroes of every giant abuser. Not every giant is a Goliath or Gargantua; nor is every mocker of giants a David. Often that which is big is great and its opposite is merely minute.

One abuse usually hurled at the Church is the charge that she has been the biggest abuser of civilization. But if Catholic abuses seem to have outnumbered all others in the world, or have seemed to do so until this century, it is because Catholicism in one way or another has been the world; at least, as great apologists have said one way or another, there have been no Mennonite parliaments, no Garibaldean monasteries, no Aboriginal universities, no Ivy League crusades, no Dervish logicians, no Doukhabor lawyers, no Laodicean controversialists, no Anarchist mission societies, no Unitarian armadas, no Vegetarian curias combing the hills of Rome. If Catholics have shown some bad taste in buildings and art, it is because Catholics more persistently than any others have built and painted. Catholicism alone has had a *Summa* because Catholicism alone is a sum. Catholicism can have laws about the smallest details of faith and morals without being pedantic because it alone can deal in generalities without getting lost.

Even Bertrand Russell, for all his meandering misperceptions, admits in an essay on teaching that dogmas universal and international clearly are not as harmful as local creeds; when there is no common civilization, the most common practice is to destroy partial civilizations. Without a universal set of truths, any remote idea is received as a wrong idea; anything foreign looms as threateningly alien, and the "universal man" of classical Catholicism with his concentric rings of natural law and divine revelation gets sort of pummeled into the "mass man" of the anti-Catholic revolutions. As a transplanted tree in a different kind of landscape can be an eyesore, so an imported idea can become a mindsore in a different kind of culture whose concept of a universal is a collective. Catholic universality is a modifying element in the contest of ideas; Puritan provincialism and Marxist internationalism alike consider it degenerate for that very reason.

Theology forces a society to be social against the inclinations of fallen man to annihilate. The Inquisition of the Spanish monarchy is a case in point. It was a cruel use of theology when it was a political program; it was a form of enlightened legal procedure unprecedented since republican Roman times when it was a theological program. While it was a blot and a stain on everything noble and pure, it caused less ruin in two hundred years than Stalin did in a few days in Eastern Europe; it was less bloody than any atheist pogrom or genocide of the modern age because its attention was wider than ideology and race; it placed ideas before ideology and the human race before races, even when its vision lacked depth to match its breadth.

The grave mistake of the Inquisitor, typical of the Spanish model and not of the Roman, was a modern mistake of confusing wrong ideas with treason. While Rome said that what is right must suit the state, Spain came close to saying that what suits the state must be right. It became modern by objecting to heresy as socially inexpedient. It lost trust in the Catholic wisdom which faults heresy for being too expedient, not for being too new. Real heresy gets to be what it is by reducing difficult universal facts to facile regional attitudes. Catholicism has objected to heresy because it is not broad enough to convince whole centuries, not because it is novel enough to convince the latest generation. The Inquisitor cast against his parched hills the first shadow of a modern form, blocking the outlines of spires and shrines and shading the scene with a new and eerie silhouette, the emerging Big Brother come to replace the Church's universal brotherhood of man.

When the Church dares to speak of wrong ideas today, editorialists instinctively point to the Inquisitor's profile, as though it were the outline of Holy Mother Church sniffing out new martyrs for science. The American press generally mocked Rome for reconsidering the judgment against Galileo; though it supported religionists who placed advertisements in the public newspapers denying the immutability of natural law in the matter of abortion. The Galileo case is ritually cited as an example of what the Church does when she meddles. But heliocentrism had the considerable praise of the scholars in the Roman College, even as they tried to give fair play to the alternative thesis of Tycho de Brahe; they gave Galileo a feast and he enjoyed the support of many hierarchs for some time without fuss; he seemed to amuse the Pope. In contrast, Melancthon and Luther had already scorned Copernicanism with violent language, and the Jesuits had given Kepler refuge in 1596 when he was ostracized by the Protestant faculty of Tübingen. When Galileo was condemned, it was for giving the impression that his ideas were upsetting the planets when in fact they were only upsetting a few professors by stating where the planets already were. Even these professors were remarkably indulgent when he proposed his preposterous theory of the tides and cast horoscopes for income. Because Galileo was a Catholic judged by Catholics, his case was a universal case, and it made no more sense to eliminate him than to eliminate the sun.

The governing principle in all the discourse was not the idolizing of the sun nor the idolizing of man, but the worship of God; the world is no more heliocentric than it is anthropocentric, because it is theocentric, and any other idea is eccentric. Galileo's science was indebted to his Christian Neo-Platonism. Heliocentrism is the physics of a monotheistic matrix. And that is why sunworshippers are foolish enough to smash up man into irrelevant bits, and that is why egoists rail against the sun. It is not that man is unimportant because he is not the sun, or that the sun is stupid because it lacks a human soul; science is safeguarded by the reasonable proposition that the worth of the womb and the worth of the world are estimated by the worth of their Creator. Galileo's only punishment was to be placed in a sunny palace where he might experiment in private; had he offended a modern court of atheists who know the worth of nothing, he might have been placed in a madhouse and experimented upon. Universal man may be wrongly judged to be wrong from time to time; mass man is liable to the worse fate of wrongly being judged to be crazy all the time. The problem with each modern bigotry is that it has not been Catholic enough to be boldly scientific. Whitehead acknowledged that. It becomes merely impetuous, like a child who smashes a clock to find out what makes it work, and is then left with only the works. We can be grateful to rare figures like Pierre Duhem and, in our own day, Stanley Jaki, who show the sources of science in Christian theism.

The more visible the Church becomes, the more she gets blamed for what she visibly is not. And still the situation is more than this: in the tremendous sweep of years and events, the Church's ubiquity makes her not so much the object of scorn as the very objectivity which provokes scornfulness itself. Palm Sunday is the paradigm of publicity, and the week it began is the sabbatical account of the way the world reports the entrance of the Divine Word into the city's gates. Whenever God publishes good news of peace, a battle breaks out: not always a raucous clash, but often a local reflex grinding against a boundless revelation. St. Vincent of Lerins defined truth as that which has been held everywhere, always and by all. The standard of universality, antiquity, and assent is the very Catholic principle of totality which the totalitarian from his modern inquisitorial shadow condemns as narrow-minded. And with the best of intentions, and with no sympathy for totalitarianism, the modern journalist may find himself repeating the same murky charges. In his desire to include all the news that fits, he may risk losing a sense of what human excellence has long revered as fitting.

The aesthetic sense which disdains the pugnacious Nativism of old-time street brawlers can be entertained by a variant of the same thing screened through television or limelighted on Broadway. "No-Popery" can have a positively enlightened ring when spoken with the refinements of major wire services and mainline syntax. The modern bigot is not a Neanderthal;

he only thinks everyone else is. But this is an injustice to primitive man who wanted to knock out his enemies' brains; the modern propagandist wants to wash them. Even journalists are not always above this. The marked rise in the form of anti-Catholic bigotry often goes unregretted and unchecked by the customary guardians of liberal discourse. Peter Viereck of Yale called it "the anti-Semitism of the liberals" and Arthur M. Schlesinger, Sr., regarded it as "the deepest bias in the history of the American people". Suburbanized bigotry is no less blunt for using the country club instead of the billy club; nor are descriptions of Catholicism less opinionated for appearing as newspaper releases instead of graffiti. To scrawl slurs on walls when no one is looking is one thing; it is another to scrawl them on minds when no one is thinking.

Professionalism

Major newspapers provide a steady stream of articles on dissident, disaffected, or lapsed Catholics, often with a glibness that makes theology a cartoon. As they are quick to cite Rome for "insensitivity" on a score of issues from morality to ecumenicism, they are no more deliberate in trying to distinguish between the Church's charism of infallibility in matters of faith and morals, and her defectibility in trying to carry them out. If a reporter discovers some bad apples in the Church, the Church will not deny it; her first sermon was about a bad apple spoiling the shining world. But the existence of a bad apple also means the existence of apples, and if apples then a tree; and the Church's second sermon is all about the tree. If a journalist does not confront the meaning of that tree, what he has to say will be as cryptic and ambiguous as the placard tacked to the top of the tree when Christ hung on it.

A journalist does not have to be a Catholic to analyze Catholic issues adequately. But theology is a science which, regardless of one's personal disposition, expects to be treated as such. It is not a game the whole family can play, unless the members of the family are theologians. And then they will not play, because they will understand why it is not a game. Commentators who do not understand the vocabulary of dogma can distort it unwittingly. When the writers are dissenting Catholics themselves, or advocates of a contrary expectation, they may well give the reader the opinions of a vested interest clothed in the supervesture of objective reporting. At times there is a poignancy about the King James translation which says that Zaccheus was unable to see Jesus "because of the press" (Lk 19:3).

Nuclear disarmament and sexual ethics, as examples, are understood by the Church to be politically and socially significant because they are theologically significant. The drama of man derives its dignity, indeed its very being, from the drama of God. Yet many secular analyses of the Church's teaching on peace and justice have ignored its fundamental anthropology, sidetracking the central place of abortion and other life issues in it. The reigning pontiff's personalist phenomenology gets reduced to what our nation's Paper of Record calls a "papal war" against women. A censured professor is declared by the same journal to be "a Roman Catholic theologian", Rome's opinion notwithstanding. A former nun is described receiving a "Wonder Woman" award for bravery against "fear" while the regular work of dutiful Religious is treated as non-existent. When a Catholic priest in a necktie spoke against the Church's decree on suitable clerical dress, and was congratulated by a Protestant clergywoman wearing a clerical collar, a news service ran the photograph with no apparent sense of the sparkling schizophrenia portrayed.

There is something about the Catholic spectacle that rattles settled minds. Its apostles have confused the philosophers since they first began preaching. Dr. Mahaffy, the Victorian professor of Greek at Trinity College, Dublin, complained of the Apostle's sermon on the Athenian hill: "Think of the impertinence of this impudent little Hebrew talking to the sages of the ancient world in that manner. I can never forgive St. Paul. There was an excellent university at Antioch, but he never seems to have availed himself of it." But so long as Catholicism does intrude upon linear civility, those who report the spectacle are obliged by their professional standards at least to acknowledge the elements of its theology. This is particularly true when journalists report division of opinion between the Church's teaching and what some in the industrial West might prefer them to teach.

The Plain Facts

One claim is clear enough: Catholic teachers with a canonical mission, chief among whom are the bishops as the official teachers of the Church, subscribe to no "Spirit of Vatican II" which is sometimes conjured up to justify eccentric conduct, but to Vatican II itself which clearly taught in *Lumen Gentium* how the episcopal office of teaching in the Church can be exercised only in communion with the Pope and members of the College of Bishops. Recalling this in an *ad limina* address to U.S. bishops (October 22, 1983), the Pope asked them to remind the world that "vigilance and fidelity on the part of bishops are synonyms for pastoral love". Obedience is legal trivia unless motivated by that love, and as the teaching voice of the Church is authentic, it requires a tough love. Quoting the Curé of Ars to bishops and priests together on Holy

Thursday in 1986, the Pope reminded them: "If a pastor remains silent when he sees God insulted and souls going astray, woe to him! If he does not want to be damned, and if there is some disorder in his parish, he must trample upon human respect and the fear of being despised or hated."

Another plain fact is that there is no such thing as an "American Catholic Church". There is the Roman Catholic Church in the United States, and any tinting of universal Catholic teaching by local presumptions is not the self-assertion of a vibrant indigenousness but a domesticated disinclination to observe precepts which transcend particular culturisms. Respective cultures promote that revealed truth through their endowed gifts by brightening, and not coloring it. In his Apostolic Letter of 1899, *Testem Benevolentiae*, Pope Leo XIII exposed the propensity of some Americans to equate the way the state works with the way Catholics believe God wants his Church to work as his Mystical Body and not as a confederation. With a zeal for national ideas which had become impatient with the subtleties of the way God pursues his children on earth, the mistake of Americanism would have replaced the primacy of such virtues as humility and obedience with social optimism and an exaggerated dependence on independence. The democracy of the enlightened seemed a thing more plausible than the mandate of the apostles, historical analysis was held suspect, and one kind of cultural enthusiasm became the measure of tenable truths. It remains capable of misgoverning many today who have been deprived of a wider cultural patrimony. Some of them mean well, which is not to say that they are right. Others perhaps more cynical would encourage it as a means of disenfranchising the Catholic Church which increasingly appeals as the remaining effective force for good in the human forum.

Another tenet has taken on new import in the heightened

complexion of these times. It is the papacy. The Pope whom God has given to his Church in this most seminal and ambivalent period of history is Polish, and it is only proper that he should be influenced by his native culture; it is even understandable that he should be an outspoken nationalist, for nationalism rightly lived as a correlative of Catholic society enhances the universal vision. But Americans, or any others, betray a thick imperiousness in assuming that he teaches what he does because of a "Polish mind-set". The same chauvinism used to complain about the papacy's "Italian mind-set". It is interesting that he is a Polish Pope; it is vital that he is a Pope. He speaks with a conviction born of a national experience and a personal suffering which few in more comfortable circumstances dare imagine. Eager participants of symposia and summer workshops should hesitate to tell him about their pain. He is gracious not to tell them of his. It would make them look like debutantes.

Instead, the Pope and his Church have a greater subject. The center of human fact is the Cross, that ghastly grace which seems to be displayed more the less it is borne, upon which the Man of All Ages was painfully pinned and which now is painlessly pinned on people. If he tells modern souls what they would rather not hear, it is only because a father is obliged to tell his family things that it might rather not hear. But he persists because the message has to do with providence; even the ancient crowd that hated the Cross because it meant something knows more about what the future provides than the modern crowd ignoring it because it means nothing.

In ample perspective, the Pope's benignity, so unlike the grimness of his frequent critics, strikes from a horizon beyond a line called the end of a flat world or the start of a round one. His voice is from a place farther east than Poland, fairly roaring from the shore of Galilee. And the good that can come out of Cracow may be the same good that came out of Nazareth.

As that old good called over the ranks of the Scribes to the crowds on coast and hillside, it now calls to perceptive intelligences and wills capable of outwitting a century's obtuseness. "When you were young, you girded yourself and walked where you would; but when you are old, you will stretch out your hands, and another will gird you and carry you where you do not wish to go" (Jn 21:18). Among the confused bystanders who thought they had engineered a New World for something called the New Man, there certainly must remain a few who are listening to this as they gaze upon the decrepitude of modernism. The journalist will write his greatest story when he can explain how the fastest growing institution of the independent age is the nursing home.

To Act Our Age

The big news for those who cover the news is that all these issues have to do with aging. A child should not be blamed for being childish; it would be like blaming a grandfather's clock for being antique. This is simply a matter of a thing acting its age. But there is a difference between acting our age, which confers dignity, and acting the way our age expects us to act, which imposes conformity. Peter Pan refused to act his age and grow up: this is infantilism. The Boy-Who-Called-the-Emperor-Naked refused to be persuaded how to act by the world: this is heroism.

While one can pretty well describe how a person should act according to the birthday coming up, it is harder to anticipate how a person should act according to the century coming up. For instance, a person entering the twenty-fifth year of his life can be expected to have certain physical and intellectual endowments, because many millions of people have already done it. But one can barely imagine what a person entering the twenty-fifth century will look and think like, because no one has done a twenty-fifth century before.

This is where history comes in, and why it is said that past is prologue. Journalism is no substitute for history, even though the electronic culture has promoted it as such. On the other hand, journalists would be better at their work if they were better at history. And to do this means avoiding historicism which, in the words of the Pope to Jesuit educators (November 9, 1985), relativizes fundamental values and "leads to an unfounded primacy of freedom over truth, practice over theory, becoming over being". What should be the sophisticated historian's *déja vu* tends to be the historicist's novelty; historicism is at heart a discreet provincialism. For one thing, reporters would relax more in their pursuit of "historical events" if they could better appreciate how there is a lot more history going on than they realize. A sane writer should be unable to think of any event that is not going to be historic tomorrow, at least until the day when time stands still.

History is the record of tradition, and tradition is the human inheritance into which various events nudge themselves and find a human place. It might dismay the journalist to realize that the historic events he wants to witness are traditional events. Only because of a tradition can words be found to describe them. Each age is unique, but the uniqueness is rooted in certain facts which permit comparison. It is uncertain whether the typical human five centuries from now will have myopia or X-ray vision; but, inasmuch as no previous century has bred cyclops, humans may be reasonably confident that their descendents will have two eyes.

The case of the Church is roughly the same. What the Church will be like five hundred years hence is also unpredictable except that, if there are five hundred more years allotted to the human race, that Church will be One, Holy, Catholic, and Apostolic. These are "marks" or constants, without which we would be dealing with a fact other than the fact of the Church, much as a biped is not a triped. The wisdom of this is the gift of tradition, and the journalist should be judicious, then, in the way he defines a traditionalist. Ranting voices which newspapers often cite as representative traditionalists are as hostile to tradition as any anarchist, and they do indeed share an impetuous regard for authority; they have little room in their economy for the factor of development which is the vehicle of tradition.

In common caricature, any change in a static world is a mutation; the "liberal" is supposed to mutilate faith and morals in the cause of change, and the "traditionalist" must then be the reactionary who resists any development, and the march of the masses is inevitably some kind of march away from the Mass. The Pope, then, appears to any members of the press who take this view as a tangle of inconsistencies, progressive on some issues and conservative on others, as though it were inconsistent to be lenient with sinners and demanding of moral theologians; or to place marriage and celibacy, social democracy and ecclesiastical hierarchy in the same shining celestial dance. If that is aberrant, so is a car travelling at different speeds on different roads. Only a behaviorist would think that, but behaviorism is very much a part of the cultural air and journalists can breathe it as nonchalantly as anyone. The behaviorist concludes that human behavior is instinctively patterned, at least more habitual than it is morally free; the behaviorist is confused by the man of integrity, and a man true to his word seems unpredictable. A man of total integrity, that is a holy man, appears totally capricious to the stern behavioral eye. The holy man disrupts the behaviorist system precisely because he is systematic about truth and serene about virtue.

There can be no *traditio,* or handing over of cultural patrimony, without motion, while the *libertas,* or moral freedom, of the classical liberal is a fixed state which secures the kinetic tradition. Subtler theorists of the nineteenth century, even if of only a deist mentality, assumed this affinity. Modern newspapers, however, confined to messages in black and white, have a tendency to think in black and white and do not discern beneath the cartoon a deep traditionalism which is less like clutching a custom and more like keeping a corpuscle. The concourse of tradition is not in a museum but in a blood bank, and finally it is in the Church where the Source of all blood is outpoured. If a journalist recognizes this, he can give credence to the schoolboy's pun about what is black and white and read all over.

He will also expect that the Church now, and again in the twenty-fifth century, will face a harsh challenge and will be given a Pope able to handle it. Observers who know the tradition have remarked how this seems to happen just about every five hundred years: Gregory I, Gregory VII, and Pius V each had their contests. Now there are those who detect a prophetic element in a line of the poet Slowacki: "A Slav Pope will sweep out the Churches and make them clean within."

Such is the intuition of many of the largest crowds ever to gather around one man. It may be that the heirs of a human race which has seen the ups and downs of five-century cycles are willing to believe in providence, or at least are willing to give space for one last attempt at the "great man" theory of history. This is not how the Pope would put it, and he has done everything possible in symbol and speech to say that the presence is not Wojtyla but a glimpse of Peter, and that the words spoken are not the conclusion of a phenomenologist but the declaration of the Cause of all phenomena. He who teaches himself, said St. Thomas, does not teach Christ.

Getting the Story Right

The papal teaching, then, cannot be without discomfort for a sentimentalist who prefers moral generalities, or for a pragmatist who envisions papal legitimacy in terms of political ideologies. It is about the kingdom of righteousness, which is not the hegemony of enlightened people. The cleansing of the churches for our salvation, which is nothing other than the purification of human hearts as they perceive God, requires the united voice of Christian truth; and although the Pope would not say that the universal teaching of Christ is fragmented (because it subsists in him as the Vicar of Christ), false doctrine is more easily believed the more true doctrine seems to be inchoate. All this may seem alien and exotic to western congressmen, midwestern merchants, and even to world-weary network news commentators, but until recently so did Afghanistan and Ayatollahs. It is neither alien nor exotic for the Church to see the world in a light more revealing than that which guides postwar materialist assumptions. In Western democracies, religious leadership has usually devolved onto persons who synthesized the lowest common denominator of spiritual inclinations. But John Paul II's concept of human regeneration is not content with the toothsome benevolence of harmless congressional prayer breakfasts; it insists on the rediscovery of the Eucharistic soul. Despite the talk of his being "the people's Pope", he would never have been elected by an American plebescite. Perhaps that is exactly why Americans are intrigued by him at a time when they can barely name most of their own officials.

It will not do for journalists to say he has been pulled by the natural course of events to fill the current vacuum of modern leaderlessness. Analysts speculate why such a likeable face should be mouthing such hard sayings. He is doing the likeliest—

though uncommon—thing for a child of God to do, and that is to speak of his Father. Politicians tend to reflect their constituencies, even sometimes against their better consciences, which is a matter of looking "through a glass darkly"; but the Pope points the people to an ikon, which is the only way to see face to face. If the universal order is in its present turmoil by a stupefying narcissism, it can get out of it only by growing out of it. And the saint on the ikon is the adolescence of Eden matured. So the Pope plows through the nations and the extravagant tumult of his own Rome like an ikon himself, relishing the rites and tongues and vestures. He even manages to look interested when a delegation of French farmers presents him with the world's largest truffle.

It would be off the mark to call it the flamboyance of an extrovert; on each of these occasions there is a core of stillness which is weightier than the absence of noise. And it becomes heavier when he kneels. As Simone Weil, the great Jew who knelt that way many times, put it: "I felt myself at the intersection of Christianity and everything that is not Christian. Withdrawal instead of making for exclusiveness, really reaches out to an inclusiveness of the universe." If there is time left to write an account of this time, the reporter might ponder as a footnote, how it was that this man who owns no clothes of his own and who wears the same outfit day by day that his predecessors have worn for centuries, should have been voted by the Fashion Institute of America, "the world's best dressed statesman".

This is an important news story, even as it daunts critics with a more limited perspective. Certainly, it is too complex for anyone to be glib about it. The universal Church now faces a combination of the challenges known to the last three epochal sets of five centuries: doctrinal dissent, internal structural dissent, and external cultural dissent. It is no time to drown in diction about an American Church flexing a fresh muscle unfelt before now. America, the Church, and the Age deserve better than that moribund thesis. A point stands out before the others: adults can act their age in a crisis by refusing to be told by their age how to act, learning to be childlike and not childish, growing wiser as the age grows more stubborn. The opposite would renew the fate of Trajan and the Antonines who, according to Gibbon, "insensibly sank into the languid indifference of private life".

Even journalists do not agree on how this is to be handled; if they did, it would reduce the number of newspapers and no one is asking for that monopoly. A good journalist, though, will understand how there is a tradition according to which a Word more than words was made flesh. And the Word was crucified by people who would not think beyond clichés. When the Word went on to make Good News, many tried to stifle the story. No one will have his own final word on this on earth, and honest journalists would be dishonest to their profession if they proposed one. But they should make an effort, and an ever honest one, to understand why the Pope and great voices in his Church are convinced that what they have long believed is more than ever believable.

III

LEGISLATING MORALITY

Morality and Moralizing

Much of religion in modern American life has been reduced to a custom of moralizing; and many Americans have come to think that religion is morality. Most religions do have a lot to say about principles of conduct, and they have said things right and wrong. But morality is not the stuff of religion, even though the sort of personality that does not want dogmas might be content if religion were merely a department in charge of moral platitudes.

Dogmatic belief colors moral exactions, it is true; the sacrifice on a Catholic altar does not make the same demands on the congregation that an Aztec sacrifice does, and an Aztec pontiff parading before his crowds is not what a Catholic pontiff believes himself to be. And this is so, not because of a difference in climate, but because of a difference between Quetzalcoatl and Christ. Moral consequences of dogma are direct and can be alarming, if your dogma says that there is a God who is appeased by ritualized surgery, or that heaven is a dream got through peyote. But while morality is a complement of dogma, it is the essence of politics. Political life may become immoral, if one dares to make such a judgment; but it can never be amoral as some religions have been. Any political action is an exercise in moral choice. To say that you cannot legislate morality is to say that you cannot legislate.

The fact is as plain as the nose on a man's face. But this is what the other man says. I have never seen my nose. My only acquaintance with it is through a mirror which gets it backwards. So I cannot see nonsense when it is *my* nonsense. Upon reflection, it looks perfectly sensible. The notion that morality cannot be legislated is plain nonsense; but it is a particularly elusive kind of nonsense for appearing so reasonable when you try to look at it. Liquor prohibition did not make America dry (although it cut drinking by one-third), and the banning of tobacco would not eliminate smoking. What seems a sensible conclusion, however, is grounded in the quicksand of absolute nonsense: namely, if some moral legislation is not advisable then none is.

A moral imperative is more than a precise religious compulsion; it is a natural human attitude. The job is to discern those basic moral principles which exist as facts of the social economy, so that we do not behave unnaturally. Moral norms are not exterior to man; they define the order intrinsic to the human condition. They are objective, inasmuch as the ontic structure of the person is ordered by natural fact and not by arbitrary predilections. And they are necessary for freedom because they conform behavior to the characteristic goods of the human being. Moral norms are those universal constants without which the essential human condition contradicts itself.

On the other hand, laws themselves are the structure of communal order and organization. They are effective only when they are assumed as its proper order by society. Moreover, they have a historical character as they adapt to the current social situation. The historical character does not compromise the objectivity of moral constants; while law and morality are separate realities, the law organizes the universal moral principles which have their play in historical development.

Nature's Ordered Whole

These things are so cogent that they hardly have had to be pointed out until recently. A sense of nature's ordered whole has been diluted by the trickle-down effects of Enlightenment philosophy, which tends either to rationalism or empiricism. In its extreme individualistic form, the dilution has produced commentary peculiar as this from the late Justice Douglas:

> Many of [the Ninth Amendment rights] in my view come within the meaning of the term "liberty" as used in the Fourteenth Amendment.
>
> First is the autonomous control over the development and expression of one's intellect, interests, tastes, and personality.
>
> These are rights protected by the First Amendment and in my view they are absolute, permitting of no exceptions.[1]

When such a view, which is not necessarily a thought, becomes a public decision, it fragments universal norms of morality into highly imperial eccentricities, now a contagion in the judiciary. Chief Justice Burger has called it "benevolent neutrality",[2] but it is a refined form of moral despotism, even when it sounds libertarian, insisting that social legislation can serve humans while shunning the universal analogy of human behavior.

The judicial posture of benevolent neutrality historically has led to an exaggeration of legalisms, lawyers, and lawsuits. This is curious, but examination shows why it is so. A mass of individuals of selective private judgment needs a lot of *ad hoc* organization, just as poor swimmers need a lot of splashing to

---

[1] *Doe v. Bolton,* 410 U.S. 179, 210–11 (1973) (Douglas, J. concurring). Cf. Francis Canavan, "The Pluralist Game" in *The Human Life Review,* IX, 3 (Summer 1983), p. 38.

[2] *Walz v. Tax Commission,* 397 U.S. 664, 669 (1970).

stay afloat. The litigious spirit always shadows "benevolent neutrality" as bureaucracy tries to fill the gap left by abandoned moral norms, as if laws secure law. But law secures laws; and by law here I speak of natural law, which is the eternal law implanted in rational creatures, guiding them to upright behavior and to their proper end.[3]

Natural Law

I do not deny that the fullness of my analysis requires that there be a God who is Creator and Legislator. St. Thomas Aquinas was certain that divine law, given in revelation, is practically necessary to clarify some universal norms (*S.Th.* I–II, q.91, q.4). But one may speak of "natural law" apart from a higher reference. Granted, it is a tiresome and rudimentary approach, and doomed to incompleteness, a point Plato makes in his correction of Protagoras.[4]

An immutable intelligence can prevent inconsistencies, such as the neurasthenic feminist's objection to pornography even as she supports sexual license. The benign neutralist fails to appreciate this: in nature's court of appeal, the offense of promiscuity and pornography alike is not that they are naked, but that they are unreasonable. Equality and romance are highly intellectual perceptions. When they are morally neutralized they become compulsive homogeneity and fantasy: moral reason concludes as a Divine Comedy, moral neutrality collapses inevitably into an autoerotic fable.

Recognition of natural law does not trivialize the social functions of laws as the pliant representations of majority will.

[3] Leo XIII, Encyclical *Libertas Praestantissimum.*
[4] *The Laws*, n. 716.

We do not need more laws so much as we need more law, just as a weak man does not need more bones, but only more backbone. And that means understanding nature. Anyone who says, "There ought to be a law", has already done a more powerful thing than a congressman can do; it is a relatively simple matter to shape a positive statute to say what ought to be, but it takes every human act since the first man and woman to shape a conscience capable of saying "ought". No man being mugged cries out for laws and orders. He rages for law and order. The bump on his head will seem more painful than the bump on the world, and he may not know that he is being victimized by the primeval exercise of Cain over Abel; but he knows enough to demand the vaster armaments of law stronger than laws and order sterner than orders. He senses what "ought" to be and is not. And by so doing, without a scrap of catechesis, he is taught by his bruises why the primitive catechists saw behind the gory kaleidoscope of sins, a pale and original molestation called Sin itself. He comes to know that history admits of certain moral principles more portentous than those autonomous spasms of the ego isolated by Justice Douglas.

It takes a breathtaking sophistication, born of an account of the human condition beyond empirical analysis, to discern sin and damnation; but the secular state is not meant to be that sophisticated. Its borders are civil and not cosmic, so it properly deals with the muted evidences of these grand realities in their domesticated forms called crime and punishment. Yet these are indications of social reality more ancestral in time and deeper in experience than conditioned reflexes. Three basic kinds of law exist: divine law (the principles of supernatural order), natural law (the principles of natural order), and human law (the principles of personal order). Positive human law does not need to allude to divine law absolutely, even though it can be clarified by a transcendent intuition; it serves its own dignity by acknowledging the brooding operation of natural law.

A theory of natural law claims to be able to identify conditions and principles of practical right-mindedness, of good and proper order among men and in individual conduct. Unless some such claim is justified, analytical jurisprudence in particular and (at least the major part of) all social sciences in general can have no critically justified criteria for the formulation of general concepts, and must be content to be no more than manifestations of the various concepts peculiar to particular peoples and/or to the particular theorists who concern themselves with those people.[5]

A False Solemnity

To discount natural law in the applications of positive law is in some way to commit the ultimate form of solipsism, the denial of the universe. That virulent unreality in one modern form, Fascism, moved Pope Pius XI to react with his universal appeal: "... the natural law is valid everywhere, 'written by the Creator's hand on the heart' (Rom 2:14), and which reason, not blinded by sin or passion, can easily read".[6] The note of reason removes any sectarianism from the fact of natural law. Natural law is an essential principle of being and not a reification.[7] Of course, most theories of natural law reach

---

[5] Clifford Kossel, "Some Problems of Truth in Ethics", *19th Jesuit Philosophical Association Proceedings,* 1957, V. James V. Schall, *Christianity and Politics* (Boston: St. Paul Editions, 1981), pp 233–34. Cf. Robert Unger in "The Critical Legal Studies Movement" in 96 *Harvard Law Review,* 563, 566–67 (1983): "If the criticism of formalism and objectivism is the first characteristic theme of leftist movements in modern legal thought, the purely instrumental use of legal practice and legal doctrine to advance leftist aims is the second."

[6] Piux XI, Encyclical *Mit brennender Sorge,* n. 35.

[7] Schall, op. cit., p. 233.

theological conclusions, and an orthodox Christian, for instance, will read in natural law specifications about artificial contraception and the indissolubility of marriage which others may not, but a conclusion is not an evidence. Evidence lies in the intuition of "oughtness": that a leader ought to be a Gandhi and not an Attila, that a right to existence ought to be and that genocide ought not to be, that to be pro-choice in a matter ought to be pro-right-choice. Autonomous attacks on this intuition do not weaken it but show its necessity. There is a wide debate about where the essentials of natural law are to be located, but that indicates a dissymmetry in the materialist vision. Whatever is essential refers to three assertions about natural goods:

> Like all substances, we tend to be, and we know that it is good to preserve and develop our being; like all animals, we tend to the preservation of the species and know that this is good; finally, we tend to the specifically human good, to know the truth about ourselves, the universe and God, and to communicate with our own peers through societal life. There is no moral precept which is not a determination of one of these essential goods; they contain in principle the totality of the human good.[8]

One can be agnostic about God and still be social; one cannot be social and be agnostic about society. The modern secularist is what he is, not because of his farsighted contempt of God who cannot be seen, but because of his shortsighted contempt of man who can be seen; he denies the rationality of natural law because he is ambiguous about human nature, and this in turn grinds out legal positivism: that is, "an error which surrounds the enactment of purely human laws with an aura of

[8] John Finnis, *Natural Law and Natural Rights* (Oxford: Clarendon, 1980), p. 18.

false solemnity and so leaves the way open for a fatal divorce of law from morality".[9]

Agnosticism about man conjures this positivist crankiness of investing laws with a significance in themselves, as if they were incantations rather than representations. A case in point is the *New York Times* analyzing child pornography in terms of a First Amendment right and agreeing with the American Civil Liberties Union and the U.S. Supreme Court that parents have no right to prevent a minor child from having an abortion. This illustrates a clarion fact: willful agnosticism about anything is not neutrality about that thing, but hostility to it. A "neutral morality" is actually a neutered morality, as representative of justice as a eunuch is a paragon of a man.

Morality in a Worldly World

In its contemporary form of secularism, agnosticism makes impartiality an unwarranted bias. An impartial judge works by scientific principles; but an impartial agnostic is guided by the most unchecked of contradictions, non-credal credalism. And so the agnostic is not impartial at all; he clearly is not impartial about agnosticism. He makes a method of unconscious dogma. When the agnostic discards universal moral norms, he abandons a unifying system of belief; but his believing quivers on like a mysterious palsy. He comes to treat law as an artifice unresponsive to the commanding facts of nature. In that case he is neither secular nor neutral, in any real sense; he is a secularist, with a habit of sciolistic coercion. A Pope condemns legal positivism specifically as a form of superstition about the

---

[9] Pius XII, Christmas Message, 1942. Cf. John XXIII, Encyclical *Pacem in Terris,* n. 47.

social order. The social danger of the secularist is that he wants to run the world by magic, for his new kind of super- stition replaces cause and effect with formula and effect. Modernity has seen its stage of several acts: the optimism of the Social Darwinists, the racism of the National Socialists, the mythic dialect of the Marxist-Leninists, and even the less theatrical magic acts of consumerism in the hedonistic West. Each is a denial of psychological fact and the economy of experience.

An Unworldly Worldliness

I am not prescribing anything other than worldliness for the world, in the Aristotelian tradition of a thing being what it is meant to be. The nemesis of secularist thought is its failure to be secular and thoughtful enough. Morality can only be lived in a worldly world, but what secularists mean by worldliness is a manifest unworldliness. Religion's complaint is against a fallen world, which means that it cannot be against a standing world; the secularist does not tell the difference, so his wisdom is dovelike and his innocence serpentine.

The secularist, claiming to be morally neutral, does not recognize how laws without natural law make a norm of normlessness. The authentic choice in justice is not between natural law and positive, punitive and statutory laws, but between natural law and unnatural law. Here is where the magic comes in, for, by way of parallel, the disruptive social debate has never really been between clerics and anti-clerics, but between clerics and wizards. Secularist neutrality in moral cases is the form of wizardry known as pragmatism: it assumes, with no physical qualification, that anything useful is a useful good. You do not need theology to grasp that, but you do need logic. And caution. Any lie can be arrived at logically if the logic starts with a lie. Nihilism is a very logical theory if you started with nothing. Thus the wise man said that "you can only find truth with logic if you have already found truth without it."

We need laws that keep the law. Laws that do not should be arrested: like the reversal of *Dred Scott* before and the reversal of *Roe* v. *Wade* to come. These decisions of the Supreme Court are instances of the "aura of false solemnity" which accompanies a willed ignorance of natural fact. A citizen of virtue does not separate the exercise of freedom according to public law and private conscience. If he pursues the "personally opposed, but . . . " line, he gets trapped in a web of perplexity. A governor, for instance, is trapped if he vetoes the death penalty as a matter of private conscience while encouraging the funding of abortions which he claims to oppose in conscience; he is trapped when he mandates the use of automobile seatbelts as a justifiable invasion of privacy, while calling abortion an inviolable private right.

The Menace of Positivism

If I have belabored natural law, it is because I do not think Americans have been adequately informed of its existence. The moral tradition in America has come to be thought of as an American moral tradition, hardly older than the philosophical attitude of the Founding Fathers, no more cosmopolitan than Philadelphia or Boston. Natural law quickened the early federal consciousness as the inheritance of a much longer tradition. This was what the U.S. Supreme Court meant as recently as 1931 in saying: "We are a Christian

people. . . . "[10] It might as well have said: "We are a people of ancient right reason"; for even the classical pre-Christian function of
law was less punitive than directive in order that a people might
be led to the attainment of the rightfully proportioned ends.

If this is right, morally non-directive discourse of any kind is
impossible. Justice Brennan's appreciation of this, in a concurring opinion on neutral values in public education, was as
defective as his understanding of autonomous and natural
rights in *Roe* v. *Wade:* he said public education can, without
prejudice to value systems, impart "a minimum amount of
information and knowledge in certain subjects such as history,
geography, science, literature, and law".[11] But Professor Paul
Vitz has recently surveyed sixty representative social study
textbooks used in U.S. public schools, and showed as Pope Leo
XIII held in the last century: "A value-free secular code does
not exist."[12] "Marriage", "husband", and "wife" are non-
existent concepts in these books; the historical roles of religion,
parents, and free enterprise are dismissed. Most of the role
models belong to one political party.[13]

The enemy menacing a pluralistic society is the liberal
positivist who uses pluralism as an excuse for promoting his
unworldly assumptions about the moral order. Any decision
to remove a human fact from public review is as much a
philosophical statement as the decision to regulate it. And one

[10] *United States* v. *McIntosh,* 283 U.S. 605, 625 (1931). Cf. Canavan,
op. cit., p. 39.

[11] *Lemon* v. *Kurtzman,* 403 U.S. 602, 655 (1971) (Brennan, J. concurring).
Cf. Canavan, op. cit., p. 46.

[12] Leo XIII, Encyclical *Humanum Genus.*

[13] Paul C. Vitz, "Religion and Traditional Values in Public School
Textbooks: An Empirical Study", The *Wall Street Journal,* December 26,
1985, p. 6.

might add, the prohibition of school prayer is an apophatic way of instituting the secularist rites; a real absence can be as palpably cultic as a real presence.

From the time of the split of the Christian West by both Reformation fideism and the Enlightenment, dysfunctional anthropocentrism has offered itself as an alternative to the sacramental theocentrism of historical Christianity. The systematic analysis of the latter has provided generous moral distinctions and legal categories without which moral legislation does easily become a species of private notions. Professor John Gueguen makes a case of our national experience:

> Compare the self-conscious and sombre legalism of Winthrop's Boston with the almost carefree political minimalism of Serra's California missions. Or compare the defensiveness of James Madison's federal republican principle with the unitary principle of hereditary authority which grounded John Carroll's aggressive apostolate. Or compare the individualistic musings of Emerson with the communitarian conscience of Brownson in the period of our great national trauma.[14]

Popular American religiosity is a direct outgrowth of the disordered individualism common to both the pietist and rationalist movements.

The kind of pluralism which that religiosity breeds cannot be reconciled with the universal moral norms which civilized law must respect. There has to be, for instance, a schematic appreciation of the difference between saloons and slavery, or between Chinese footbinding and Eskimo euthanasia. One function of positive law is to instruct in that moral architecture. The question cannot be one of law requiring a man to act as a

---

[14] John A. Gueguen, "Public Morality in Liberal Democracy", *Proceedings of the Eighth Convention of the Fellowship of Catholic Scholars,* 1985, p. 57.

theist; it should compel him to act as a man. There is no neutrality in this, but neither is it sectarian, since the human race is not a sect nor is the ordered universe a denomination. If "no one has the right to impose his morality on anyone else", everyone has the duty to allow nature to impose its morality on everyone else.

What passes for a pluralism of conventions in the West exposes a society alienated from its nurturing sources, divorcing scientific psychology from any animating integrity. As a complex it removes the human personality from the effective significance of life and death, and reduces justice to an engine of unstable pragmatism. Consider the national reaction to the recent explosion of the space shuttle *Challenger*. One rare editorialist, fed up with the bathos and media manipulation (from the tabloids screaming "A Nation on Its Knees" to the *New York Times* giving the incident more full-page coverage than it gave any single episode of World War II), had the courage to write: "So we had many words about trauma and catharsis coming together, as if we are an animal pack facing unknown night, or as if we had seen for the first time the skull beneath the flesh and needed treatment for an inexplicable chill. There was hugging and there were tears and counselling and confession of feelings, and the end result was that we were supposed to feel better."[15]

Universal concepts, which provided the substance of a sense of justice and order, have yielded to a civil theosophy which mingles a remnant language of eternity with a suburbanized Epicureanism aimed only at "self-actualization". School children innocently wearing party hats and blowing horns as a spaceship takes off are part of the rambunctious pageant of discovery; when they suddenly see death on the television,

---

[15] Frank Morriss in *The Wanderer*, 119: 7, February 13, 1986, p. 4.

they are made part of a more portentous fact. If they are just led into grief-trauma therapy, they could become more neurotic than their teachers. It is not enough to croon Maeterlinck's line, "There is no death"; the absurdity will soon mean that there is no life. The child's isolation becomes the habit of the adolescent and the philosophy of the adult, like a blanket to breathing when applied to moral consciousness. But such is the offering which replaces transcendent perception; it is a religion of the self even when it does not seem a religion to itself. It claims to be an alternative to religion when it is only an alternative to reality. And as such it becomes that confused and disproportionate kind of morality known as moralism, a form of ethics wrenched away from disciplines of metaphysics, substituting mawkishness for mercy because it has no litmus for justice. The more moralistic it is, the more inclusive it claims to be; you can have as many moralistic exhortations as you want once the integrity of the norm is abolished. It would be less cruel if it were less sentimental.

In contemporary idiom, the finest attribute of the modern liberal, or positivist, mood is its sympathy; its worst fault is its lack of empathy. Liberalism of the modern statist school is incessantly reforming and hardly transforming in the classical way of educating the passions. It invents programs, then does not know why or how to program the inventions. The liberal lawmaker is precisely that and only that; if he better understood the etiology of behavior as a participant, and were not so confident as an observer that behavior is a reflex to an environment, he would be more of a lawgiver. The lawgiver, aware of the chemistry between natural law and human law, uses civil statutes as functions of the primal facts of life and living, the natural norms without which the lawmaker is little more than a legal lawbreaker. In unwitting tribute to this, the legalist who says that you cannot legislate morality makes a crusade of legislating immorality. If you shatter the principle of universal norms, you may actually find yourself declaring that a crippled baby does not have a right to life or that a crime against nature is an alternative way of expressing nature.

Universal Laws and Plural Values

What seems, in the name of pluralism, to be a panoply of ethical discourse, like the component colors of a spectrum, is a disintegration of substantial ethics altogether, like the smashed bits of Humpty Dumpty. Natural law secures the complementary social bonds of uniqueness and universality; to abandon it is to separate the part from the whole. Society does not then return to a prelapsarian innocence. It rushes headlong into an unnatural flux in which individuation becomes isolation and universality an unlovely communalism.

On Vice and Virtue

The problem of plural standards will not be resolved to the satisfaction of anyone who denies the educative function of the law, nor will any accommodation satisfy an undue Platonic rigidity about abstract norms. St. Thomas did propose some kind of resolution; he did not insist that all vices be proscribed or that all virtues be prescribed. He takes a minimalist position, having inherited the bounty of St. Augustine's practical outlook which mitigated the classical idealism:

> Law is laid down for a great number of people, of which the majority have no high standard of morality. Therefore it does not forbid all the vices, from which upright men can keep away,

but only those grave ones (*sed solum graviora*) which the average
man can avoid, and chiefly those which do harm to others and
have to be stopped if human society is to be maintained, such as
murder and theft and so forth (*S.Th.,* I–II, q.96, a.2).

As he assumes assent to norms, St. Thomas does not allow
options about such essential assaults as abortion and euthanasia.
The latitude obtains in the question of vices. Here the standard
is prudential: not whether or not there is such a thing as vice,
or whether or not it should be suppressed, but whether or not
a law suitably educates a people against it. Justice is served by
timeliness: "The purpose of human law is to bring people to
virtue, not suddenly, but step by step" (*S.Th.* I–II, q.96, a.2).

The totality of virtue cannot be effected by statute. Human
law has a limited obligation to make men good within the civil
order; much of morality is beyond its competence. But, all
virtues have social implications as they secure freedom, and so
political laws must not obstruct them, even when they cannot
positively enforce them. Likewise, vice is to be opposed pru-
dently as a threat to freedom which is the ground of justice.
Thus Alexander Pope:

> Vice is a monster of so frightful mien,
> As to be hated, needs to be seen,
> Yet seen too oft, familiar with her face
> We first endure, then pity, then embrace.

As for the crimination of sin, a sin according to divine law
should be made a crime in human law only if it trespasses the
public principles of life established by natural law. Here recurs
the principle of proportion: *lex non curat de minimis.* It is in
light of this, and not out of respect to privacy, that sexual
ethics are treated. Sexuality is the most public of realities, and
when veiled is most visible. The bedroom may be the most
private room in the house but it is also the most public room in

the nation; neither the kitchen nor the study nor the dining room produces populations. Positive law applies to so public an institution in a very limited way, and intervenes in the interest of consistency: when, for example, those who insist that no law should restrict an unnatural sexual practice because it is private, try to publicize that practice. Law is obliged to invoke its censures against any attempt to make its educational role a tool of propaganda promoting disordered appetites and affections. The more the image of the natural is effaced by prurient television programs and other public entertainments, the more necessary are restrictions. This is not an instance of the law invading the bedroom; it is to prevent the bedroom from invading the law.

> Now we have seen that the law is ordained to the common good, and consequently there is no virtue of which some activity cannot be enjoined by law. Nevertheless human law does not enjoin every act of virtue, but those acts only which serve the common good, either immediately, as when the social order is directly involved from the nature of things, or mediately, as when measures of good discipline are passed by the legislator to train citizens to maintain justice and peace in the community (*S.Th.*, I–II, q.96, a.3).

Much immorality has been foisted upon the community by misguided attempts to legislate the good. One reason for this is that the greatest issues tend to attract both the greatest and smallest minds. Greatness states the obvious to make it an axiom; pettiness to make it an excuse. In the analogue of justice, the vital issues are most quickly discerned by exceptionally broad minds and uncommonly narrow minds. The prophet and the pedant have the same subject; they differ only in the predicate.

I would locate moral pedantry, at least as much as anywhere

else, in the secularist prejudice which allows, and even urges, regulation of activities which it considers public, such as economic justice, while leaving the individual to decide as a matter of private right anything that does not conform to the progressivist agenda; which says religious leaders were prophetic in the civil rights movement and are meddlesome in the pro-life movement. Strictly speaking, there are no private moral matters, unless they are pathologies. Anything moral is human and, by definition, impinges on the social order. The application of law depends on the possibility of practical public regulation. But the imposition of order in itself does not compromise moral freedom; quite the opposite, it motivates it, since the one free conscience is that which has been formed by reason. And similarly, it is not possible to isolate social sin from personal sin: social sin is personal sin on a large scale, and to speak as though social sin were an autonomy is just verbal magic. This means, then, that to legislate in the social order without reference to the private sector is as realistic as guarding against a nuclear explosion without guarding the atom.

Once again, the strategy is so apparent that it goes unnoticed by those who make no distinction between a big thing and an important thing, between a grandstand and a great stand. There are the macro-moralists who would disarm a violent nation without disarming a violent citizen; who would preserve an endangered whale while shredding an endangered baby; who would call a free market perverse and free love a virtue. The mistake is the confusion of free will and freedom. A civil act can secure the grounds for freedom by declaring freedom from vice, but the one valid declaration of freedom is a form of indenture to the laws of virtue. The specificity of the laws is a matter of discussion, but the conversation should be more than gratuitous. After all, a utopia is a hell built by sheer kindness. It is inhuman to be merely humane; proper law should teach people to be positively human.

The state closest to a benevolent utopia may have been Paraguay when it was governed by the Society of Jesus in the seventeenth and eighteenth centuries. But if it was something close to heaven on earth, it was such only because its governors well taught how far earth is from heaven. The Jesuits in those days regarded kindness as virtuous, but kindness as an exclusive principle was to them a patronizing mannerism, like sanitizing a man instead of sanctifying him. The missionaries in Paraguay were emphatically not what an ordinary altruist would call uplifting, because they knew a lofty truth: human stature is not a matter of altitude, but it has much to do with attitude. Or to be more precise, the height of any reformation of society's morals is measured by the depth of the transformation of the moral society. The Jesuits would have been puzzled by any injunction to be "natural" with the Guarany Indians simply because, in the spiritual hierarchy, they intended one day to kneel before some of them and call them saints. Their utopia was not hellish because it was not utopian: the priests built it as a place to leave for heaven. If an earthly paradise is an end in itself, it is a dead end, and all its laws are traps. Kindness is an infernal machinery without something of heaven in it, and when what is called the pure milk of human kindness gets mixed up in it, it curdles quickly. Utopianism does not recover kind innocence; it certainly does expose unkind ignorance. To restore an Eden is only to revert to nudity; and to go back to the Noble Savage is stupidly to turn away from the Servant of God.

This, then, is also a guide for legislating the truth. We need a realistic understanding of how to correct ignorance. We are men and not angels, it is true; not because there are no angels, but because angels are angels and men are men. Modern moralists began to reshape their philosophy of law as though people, and not angels, are angels. Anyone who denies original sin believes that one way or another. The theologians call the notion angelism; the modernist calls it humanism. But it is totally useless for getting a realistic picture of what is to be done by law. The Kingdom of Heaven can be within us only if there is a Kingdom of Heaven outside us in the first place; it is the model for the moral life on earth, not because we are angels but precisely because we are not. Altruistic social engineers need a blueprint greater than themselves, or else they may become social buccaneers whose blueprint is themselves. Many conclusions can be drawn from modern social experiments, but one stands out clear before any other: no one is less useful to civil good than the civil utilitarian. He is the one thorough utopian, and the one thorough failure.

Now, the President of the United States is not the Pontifex of a civil religion, nor are the justices superannuated Votaries and Vestals. If they pretended to be such, they would be laughed out of the courts and congresses, for they would look awkward and silly; excellence at ceremonies, even empty ones, is not an American characteristic. But they are guardians of a flame nonetheless. There are times when Mr. Lincoln may be Father Abraham, and there are occasions when juridical robes may be donned as vestments. These are when the flame is blown about and in danger of going out. Yet a Pontifex may read the auguries a wrong way, and the black robes may seem like shrouds. It happens when the flame of human life is declared to be a thing other than moral life. If the state is not *custos morum,* it is some sort of *custos,* if not of the law of morality then of the life of morality. If that law is left unread, and that life goes unprotected, the normative light of human behavior flashes into a thousand little brushfires known to the weary conscience as legalisms and moralisms.

Mental fatigue may call this moral progress, but it is the

formula of a destructive alchemy which can declare a baby unreal and killing a mercy; which can turn two sexes into one and the one into two. Positive law cannot legislate all morality, even in the name of an order higher than this secular trance; but legislators do safeguard and promote essential goods commonly discerned by integral reason and selfless will, or else they demoralize the legislation, the legislated, and themselves. The most demoralized people think that anything legal is moral. This is not legislated morality, nor is it unlegislated morality; it is that humane fantasy which the truly human know to be legalistic moralizing.

IV

THE CONSCIENCE OF
THE PUBLIC CATHOLIC

A Sad Necessity

The *New York Times* has expressed the opinion that abortions performed on teenaged mothers are not only a "necessity" but are indeed a "sad necessity". Now if this is not an outright ascetical judgment, it is at least an aesthetical judgment somehow rooted in a remnant morality. Not even a secular editor can evade the shadow of inherited intuitions; shadows disappear only at high noon and our civilization is manifestly more in the afternoon of social coherence, when shadows are longest.

The editor did not shy from a deeper entanglement with morality. He meandered the farthest length of the shadow, then looked up and announced that "unintended pregnancies" tend to strike "victims of contraceptive failure, ignorance, and innocence". This is a breathtaking triad of afflictions. If the words seem to hiss, it is not air escaping from a syllogism; it is a more portentous sound from Paradise-Being-Lost. Adam was Blithe Adam until his Eve heard the hiss: "Victims of innocence". The primeval lie was mean for Man and Woman and for all men and women, and it was uncomfortable for the Misinformer who was condemned to crawl out of a garden of good into a jungle of good and evil, with little support for his confusion of innocence with naiveté other than a forthcoming few pillars of society and a couple of columns on the editorial page of the *New York Times*.

People, not even modern people, get their morality from editors. If laws graven by God's hand are flaunted, it is unlikely that newsprint will always be read and obeyed. Morality has to have something atmospheric about it to work. It should be less like the weather and more like the climate. If it is to be liveable and breathable, it has to be absorbed without notice; otherwise, it becomes a form of etiquette which easily turns into a comedy, or tragedy, of manners. Moral reality can be violated; it cannot seriously be questioned by a healthy mind, just as one does not think about which foot to place on the next step unless one is in physical therapy. But civilization has had the equivalent of a paralyzing stroke—its clinical name is the Twentieth Century— and the basic references for moral progress have to be learned all over again. This takes patience, even as newspaper editors trip over their own syntax.

The Modern Paralytic

The first steps of progress are not easy after an attack of modernity, because part of the modernist affliction is the loss of memory. It does not suffice to say morality must be like the atmosphere if you have no recollection of pure air. If you inhale enough smog you may even feel victimized by your first gasp of clarity. Some Twentieth Century people cannot slow down without fast food, or quiet themselves without background music. When you have forgotten how to dine and listen, you need all the help you can get just to eat and hear. In the amnesia, garden flowers come to remind us of wax ones, and babies look like imitations of expensive dolls. If the Modern Paralytic were to be told, "Take up your bed and walk", he would take it to mean that he could not have a car. All of us have heard some traumatized sociologist or clergyman claim that subway graffiti is an art form. And when they see a clean wall they think it an empty wall, another victim of innocence.

There have been enough accounts of Religious leaving their convents for government jobs to indicate a loss of social memory even among those who were consecrated to conserve it. The sad mix-up will be exposed in some future survey of these years for what it really is: the last struttings of a clericalism which thought the world was its cloister. If we walk that way, when someone says, "What you have come to represent is not the mind of Catholicism", we would probably reply, "I prefer the air I can see to that invisible air, my graffito to that illumination, my think-tank to old Ravenna or older Rome." Then, without attending a reaction, we could proceed to decry air pollution, illiteracy, and isolationism.

Being so bewildered, it is hard to remember that Religious were intended to communalize common sense and then pass it on to the world. The constant burden of Vatican II's decree on Religious Life, *Perfectae Caritatis,* was to place Religious at the disposal of the laity, not to laicize the clergy or to clericalize the laity, but to place both in a cooperative economy in which the laity would bring the detachment cultivated by the clergy and Religious into the daily existence proper to the marketplace. When Catholics live according to this order, there are immensely practical results. But the uncommon evidence of common sense among Catholics who try to be "in dialogue with the world" shows that, once innocence is thought to be naive and the Misinformer a source of information, then only the naive are thought innocent and only the Misinformer is considered informed; and the vast system of Catholic social polity breaks up and scatters among nervous activists who are of the world but not really in it.

Tension between the interior life of the soul and the public life of the world is resolved as the Catholic discerns in temporal existence a vocation to "istence"; that is, as Pope John Paul II said in a speech to UNESCO (June 2, 1980): "Man, who in the visible world is the only ontic subject of culture, is also its only object and its term. Culture is that through which man as man, becomes more man, 'is' more, has more access to being." Human detachment from worldliness is the one sovereign attachment to the world. Vatican II made it a point:

> the layman actively inserts himself into the very reality of the temporal order and takes his part competently in the work of the world. At the same time, as a living member and witness of the Church, he brings its presence and its action into the heart of the temporal sphere (*Apostolicam Actuositatem*, n.29).

The Catholic Politician

Given this imperative, is there a barrier in American society against the Catholic politician who does not intend to compromise his Catholicism in the exercise of official public duty? How dense is the wall of separation between Church and State? Or is there one at all? The separation is not a constitutional principle. It was coined as a term in a letter of Thomas Jefferson whose own applications of it do not indicate that he thought it meant anything other than what is indeed a constitutional principle: namely, that Congress should not prefer one institutionalized formula to another in stating the transcendent circumstances of the human condition. That spirit of equanimity is also a spirit of commitment to the virtues of natural law structuring the public welfare. So George Washington used his Farewell Address to advise that politics and morality must never be separated. The religion clauses of the First Amendment provide for both nonestablishment and free exercise. The Supreme Court's resolution of these in modern times has been clumsy and ambiguous.

Having abandoned the metaphysics of innocence to embrace the physics of naiveté, liberal idealism of the nineteenth and twentieth centuries assumed that socially constructive obedience to natural law would remain a habit of civilized people. John Stuart Mill, in *On Liberty,* for instance, had little doubt that the Mormon practice of polygamy would be overwhelmed by a wider social wisdom; in practice, the opposite has taken place as nearly half of all Americans now practice polygamy in its consecutive form of divorce and remarriage. But his confidence seems abjectly supine when you substitute for polygamy a more elementary distortion of ontology, such as contraception or abortion or euthanasia, the very mention of which would have offended his classical liberality:

> A recent writer, in some respects of considerable merit, proposes (to use his own words) not a crusade, but a *civilizade,* against this polygamous community, to put an end to what seems to him a retrograde step in civilization. It also appears so to me, but I am not aware that any community has a right to force another to be civilized. So long as the sufferers by the bad law do not invoke assistance from other communities, I cannot admit that persons entirely unconnected with them ought to step in and require that a condition of things with which all who are directly interested appear to be satisfied, should be put an end to because it is a scandal to persons some thousands of miles distant, who have no part or concern in it. Let them send missionaries, if they please, to preach against it; and let them, by any fair means (of which silencing the teachers is not one), oppose the progress of similar doctrines among their own people. If civilization has got the better of barbarism when barbarism had the world to itself, it is too much to profess to be afraid lest barbarism, after having been fairly got under, should revive and conquer civilization.

Modern social pragmatism has relocated the primacy of natural law, so that it is hard to distinguish between moral cases in a coherent order. It will not do, from the ground of natural law, to equate polygamy or some such other social offence with abortive and contraceptive procedures or forced sterilization or euthanasia or nuclear annihilation which do not meet Mill's criteria for exclusion from civil application; he says there should be no *civilizade* when no victim asks for help, and when the scandal is distant. In the deep matters, the victim cannot ask, and the scandal is immediate, having been condoned by federal jurisprudence. But he does consider the case of a civilization which does not prevail over incivility, and his judgment, though inadequate, is sobering:

> A civilization that can thus succumb to its vanquished enemy, must first have become so degenerate that neither its appointed priests and teachers, nor anybody else, has the capacity, or will take the trouble, to stand up for it. If this be so, the sooner such a civilization receives notice to quit, the better. It can only go on from bad to worse, until destroyed and regenerated (like the Western empire) by energetic barbarians.

A spark of Mill's confidence in perduring humanism motivated some modernized Christian social theory. In England of the 1920s, William Temple's Conference on Christian Politics, Economics, and Citizenship was too impractical to move from page to praxis; and later in the United States, John Courtney Murray's dialogue concept was too frail to survive the various misapplications of his often ignored dictum: "The Catholic may not, as others do, merge his religious and his patriotic faith, or submerge one in the other. He must reckon with his own tradition of thought, which is wider and deeper than any that America has elaborated."

The ensuing wave of sentimentality, always the consequence

of ebbing doctrinalism, had a kind of symbol for itself in a painting still on sale in some church supply shops, and to this day no one behind the counter probably thinks it silly: it is the picture of Pope John XXIII and President John Kennedy carrying baskets and sowing seeds as they walk together through a field toward a horizon on which looms, not the Heavenly Jerusalem, and not even Old Jerusalem, but the glass tower of the United Nations. The Pope in his white silk soutane looks removed far enough from his Bergamo farm to seem awkward; and the President, elegantly tailored, has the air of a man doing one more thing to please his wife. More daunting is the prospect that these two most important Catholics in consort, if they do not stop, are about to land in the East River.

Catholics who hold responsible positions in public life will not help make the Church "the salt of the earth" until they outgrow that scene. For one thing, it does injustice to the spiritual wisdom of John XXIII whose image has been manipulated by the same sort of caricaturists who turned St. Francis of Assisi into a pious leprechaun: Pope John knew that the border of the Promised Land was not along the FDR Drive. But it also tints the circumspection which muted the Kennedy idealism and shaped its essentially Hegelian observance of a commanding order of principles higher than absolute morality. There must be some significance in the broad curiosity of historians about the Catholicity of the Kennedy family and the rare consideration of any spirituality about the first Catholic president himself. A certain bias against Catholic credalism may be at the source, as it persists in portraying Catholicism as an ancestral endowment rather than as a personal commitment.

Governor Alfred E. Smith was a more reliable example of the Catholic politician. He was not a candidate who happened to be a Catholic, but a Catholic who happened to be a candidate. This of course may explain why he was not elected. He explained his Catholic commitment as a Catholic should: with serious respect for the dignity of his cultured despisers, with the same respect for his uncultured despisers, and with greater respect for the logic of Catholic systematics.

His open letter to Charles C. Marshall in the *Atlantic Monthly* (May 1927), written with the collaboration of Father Francis Duffy, is a model of canonical and theological exposition. Another essay, delivered as a speech at Oklahoma City (September 1928) is no less recondite for being a response to a Baptist publication which had accused him of drunken driving down Broadway at fifty-six miles an hour. He does not blush to cite the Catholic convictions of two Chief Justices, Roger Brooks Taney and Edward Douglas White, and is not even adverse to mentioning the word sin in a context which is not without relevance to Catholic politicians today: "A sin of omission is sometimes as grievous as a sin of commission."

The apologetic, let us confess, is far from that of John Kennedy delivered to the Protestant ministers in Houston during his presidential campaign when, against Constitutional warrant, he was subjected to a religious test. This is a sensitive contention to any who have swallowed the camel of recent social myth; and it may threaten any modern Catholics whose ideal was a New Frontier Camelot. But a fair analysis should illustrate that Kennedy, undoubtedly with the best intentions, was bidding for an Erastian settlement far more congenial to the accommodating spirit of Frederick II or Mazarin than to the prophetic impulses of Pope John. It is evident, and understandably so, that John Kennedy did not seem driven like Hilaire Belloc who waved his rosary before a Protestant heckler when campaigning for Parliament; it is also evident, and less understandably so, how he felt obliged to assure the Houston audience that his Catholicism would not compromise his affinity for liberty. The claim is innocuous until it is compared with

Smith's insistence that Catholicism rightly lived would enhance his libertarian commitments, being the core of Western culture. Kennedy's Houston speech did not mark Catholicism come of age, nor even Catholicism coming of age, but it was a species of Catholicism reluctant to tell its age. Its eclectic cadences signalled a breakdown in systematic apologetic, opening the field to various Catholics in politics today who imagine a civil need to distance themselves from the ordinary episcopal magisterium as they promote party platforms which appeal to isolated special interests even as they contradict Catholic anthropology. From the time of the Kennedy campaign, it has been easier for a Catholic to be in public life, but it has been harder than ever for a Catholic to be Catholic in public life.

The Myth of Neutrality

If we recognize the difference between the German concept of *Kultur,* or civilization, which is an inclusive structure of institutions and norms crystallizing a philosophical climate, and the classical practice of *paideia,* or culture as the devoted pursuit of knowledge for its own integrity, we can then anticipate how a civilization without such culture is contradictory and self-destructive. In politics this boils down to the contrast between the Periclean ideal of the educated man which Al Smith, who boasted having been an alumnus of the Fulton Fish Market, was not restrained by pedantry from resembling, and the modern technocrat politician whose perception of the common good is reduced to an admixture of sentimentalism and cynicism. The classicist will contradict the current romantic images, for instance, as he detects in the human and urban sturdiness of Al Smith a thing more valued by the Greek peripatetics and poets than by more recent and popular Catholic politicians whose style is less humane for being self-consciously urbane, and whose rhetoric, typically a seriatim compendium of secondary sources, seems cultured to those who in their civility have lost their culture.

It does not readily occur to the technocrat to pursue the metaphysical question behind all social problematics: "What do we believe we are dealing with when we deal with a human?" But the far different public figure according to Plato, or Dante for that matter, would not undertake the administration of human welfare without being as careful in his consideration of the human as he is in his perception of what made him fare well. The most useless public figure is the utilitarian who does not address humans when he addresses humanity; without humans, after all, humanity would be conspicuously vacant. Any estimable assessment of the human condition has to be religious if it is to avoid the doublespeak which tries to improve the quality of life by eliminating lives.

Monsignor Josemaria Escrivá wrote: "Nonsectarianism. Neutrality. Those old myths that always try to seem new. Have you ever bothered to think how absurd it is to leave one's Catholicism aside on entering a university or a professional association or a scholarly meeting or Congress, as if you were checking your hat at the door?" But so persistent is the religious imperative, that hostility to it becomes a religion of its own. The most demanding new religions have been those of Lenin, Hitler, and Mao Tse-Tung. The practice of secularizing humanism is as unnatural as the practice of splitting atoms, and the moral result is as explosive. This means that while Church and State may be separate, they must not be split; the rupture of the social from the transcendent eliminates the possibility of a functioning culture. Pope John XXIII wrote in *Pacem in Terris* of the diminishing influence of Christianity on modern society: "It is our opinion that the explanation is to be found in the inconsistency in their mind [i.e., of Christians] and their action in the temporal sphere." This passage appears in Sigrid Undset's life of Saint Catherine of Siena:

> The artificial division of religion and politics did not exist for the people of the Middle Ages. If they thought over the matter at all, they were completely aware that all the problems concerning the community—good or bad government, the welfare or misery of the people—are in the final instance religious problems. . . . If a man loves God, he will be able to love his neighbor, to attain wisdom, and to be just and truthful. Because God is our eternal blessedness, a child of God becomes a blessing for his fellows. Love for one's own ego, for something which is in reality nothing, leads to an abyss of nothingness. The love of a selfish man is nothing, truth escapes between his hands, his wisdom will show itself to be foolishness, his justice injustice, and in the end a series of disappointments and mistakes will lead him to hell—to the devil who is the spirit of disappointment and barrenness.

The present social order, as it lacks such unity, does not abandon the attempt at human acts, but it does create an inconsistent policy for determining what they should be. It is hardly an advance, and it is in fact a retreat of the human effort toward peace, justice, security, and order. This must certainly be the explanation for one politician enjoining the elderly to "die and get out of the way". The idea was so regressive that when the *New York Times,* the voice not to be ignored, said that "his mind was in a decent place", it had to hark back to the wisdom of Homer to justify such pagan fatalism: " . . . one generation of man will grow while another dies". But if editorial writers choose to comb the lawns of Ionia, they should bear in mind, as Hippolytus warned about the typology of the pseudonymous Simon Magus (*Philosophumena,* 6:14), that selective citation of the *Iliad* is as quirky as the similar mining of the

Scriptures of the Jews. More poignant would have been the words which Homer placed on Priam's lips: "Think of thy father, godlike Achilles, and pity me. He is old, as I am, and, it may be, his neighbours trouble him, seeing that he has no defender. . . . " Or, given the editor's impression of agile acquaintance with the Dorian sagas, he should not have overlooked that place in the *Odyssey* where Ulysses tells Antinoüs: "It is hard for an old man to fight with a young. Yet will I do it." If a writer has decided that there is more authority in Attic myth than in salvation history for his public recommendations, he should at least explain why he thinks this is so; for it is a moral judgment of consequence to a world which has lived long beyond the ancient odysseys to know that no one, especially not the Perfect Model of the adventurer with blood stirred in him, glided gently into the mute underworld.

This is a knowledge particularly in the possession of the Christian who knows about a Good Friday death which was as foolish to the Greeks as it was scandalous to the Jews. The foundational documents of the United States were not oblivious to it in any final degree, and consequently, a figure in a position of public trust is obliged to secure a vision of life and death which is more providential than fatalistic; he should deliberately do so when it is obscured in the public statutes. Pope John Paul II was speaking not only to Catholics when he said in his message for the 17th annual World Day of Social Communications (June 3, 1984): "The same public power which is rightly interested in the physical health of its citizens has a duty to provide with diligence, through promulgation of laws and their effective application, to see to it that there be no grave damage to public morality." And what, one is bound to ask, can be graver than a damage which leads to the grave?

An Economy of Moral Associations

The enemy of the rightly ordered moral life is to be located in
the secular form of egocentrism which has developed in consequence of the individualism of the various Protestant and
Enlightenment movements, driving a dualist wedge between
the private and public moral constructions. Through indirect
Latin influences, Jefferson had succeeded remarkably in pre-
serving for his federal declarations a Thomistic wholeness
which not even his deism had the comprehension to wipe out.
To say one cannot judicate morality is to say one cannot
judicate anything at all. English common law, for example,
actually adapts ecclesial definitions in the parallel concepts of
felonies and misdemeanor crimes in civil law, and mortal and
venial sins in moral law.

This relationship is simply not understood when the entire
economy of moral associations is rejected. One Catholic politician has said in published reports that the regulating principle
for him in all actions public and private is his conscience. This
affirms the fundamental Catholic guide to human acts, but it
parts company with orthodoxy when it ignores the obligation
to inform the conscience, concluding that the private conscience does not have the privilege of public representation. As
for the first error, there is helpful recourse to what Cardinal
Newman wrote in his Letter to the Duke of Norfolk in 1874:

> The rule and measure of duty is not utility, nor expedience, nor
> the happiness of the greatest number, nor State convenience,
> nor fitness, order and the *pulchrum.* Conscience is not a long-
> sighted selfishness, nor a desire to be consistent with oneself; but
> it is a messenger from Him who, both in nature and grace,
> speaks to us behind a veil, and teaches and rules us by His
> representatives. Conscience is the aboriginal Vicar of Christ, a
> prophet in its informations, a monarch in its peremptoriness, a

priest in its blessings and anathemas, and even though the eternal priesthood throughout the Church could cease to be, in it the sacerdotal principle would remain and would have a sway (*Diff.* II, 248–249).

And for the second proposition, that the conscience has public access only when it is a statement of manifest individualism, a private opinion disclosed rather than an interior conviction externally disposed, Newman says a bit later:

> Conscience has rights because it has duties; but in this age, with a large portion of the public, it is the very right and freedom of conscience, to ignore a Lawgiver and Judge, to be independent of unseen obligation. It becomes a license to take up any or no religion, to take up this or that . . . to boast of being above all religions and to be an impartial critic of each of them.

Newman spoke familiarly to a civil structure which had often been at odds with Catholic morality. Conscience had its valiant play from the start of the divorce between Church and State in moral formulations, when Saint Thomas More had vowed: "I never would pin my soul to another man's back." Unlike others for whom the silence of consent satisfied guilt, he recognized the limits of a passive conscience in the exercise of public duty. It cost him more than an election or preferment. It cost him his breath. We would not say it cost him his life, for in fact it extended his life to the length of eternity: "I die the King's good servant. But God's first."

The press has told of one intelligent Catholic, prominent in national politics, who, having announced for higher office, removed a portrait of St. Thomas More from his study, saying that it made his non-Catholic associates uncomfortable. It was not the first time the saint had his head removed; but while in Tudor times the loss of one's head signalled the end of a career, it has come in these late democratic times to be a requirement for starting one.

When a Catholic public figure gives the impression of wanting no more of Mr. More, even when this is probably not his actual disposition, it almost appears that the saint has stopped interceding and started haunting. For it must be remembered that the saint rendered more to Christ than to Caesar. Especially troublesome, necessarily more so to the Catholic for whom he is a saint than to others for whom he may be a heroic anachronism, are More's words on the association between personal conscience and objective conscience in the external forum. In the ubiquitous dank of the Tower of London, he brightly told his daughter Margaret: "I know my own frailty full well and the natural faintness of my own heart, yet if I had not trusted that God should give me strength to endure all things than to offend him by swearing against my own conscience, you may be sure that I would not have come here." His obedience is to that "aboriginal Vicar of Christ" which does not part from the truth pronounced by the Vicar of Christ himself, however much one might distance oneself from Rome, as both are instruments of the Author of immutable natural law. So St. Thomas More concluded: "I believe, when statesmen forsake their own private conscience for the sake of their public duties . . . they lead their country by a short route to chaos." Alas, in a published interview, Senator Edward Kennedy said, in his estimation, Thomas More had been "intolerant".

The public Catholic is in a position to limit offenses against the natural law which must be regarded as the social standard, and not an arbitrary interior affinity, if civilization is not to diminish culture. Solzhenitsyn presented morality as the evidence of natural law autonomous among all laws:

Morality is higher than law! Law is our human attempt to somehow embody in rules a part of that moral sphere which is above us. We try to understand this morality, bring it down to earth and present it in the forms of laws. Sometimes we are successful, sometimes less so. Sometimes you have, in fact, a caricature of morality, but morality is always higher than law, this view must never be abandoned (Speech to the AFL-CIO, 1983).

There has not been a change in the Catholic policy which recognizes this, nor in the Catholic insistence on promoting it by cultivating all the natural virtues as they are rooted in the primary ones of prudence, justice, temperance, and fortitude. But the same Catholic governor who no longer looks upon the face of Thomas More, recently took to the pulpit of a non-Catholic church to explain Catholicism's strengths and weaknesses as he understands them. In particular, he stated that there have been "two Catholic Churches", one Pre-Vatican II and one Post-Vatican II. From the purview of inspiration, this is tantamount to the resolution of the mock innocent abroad who, having been shown two skulls of Alexander the Great, decided that one must have been Alexander as a boy. Not content to leave it at that, the speaker insisted that the Pre-Vatican II Church had been largely occupied with "weeding out those who were unfit for the joys of heaven", while the Post-Vatican II Church provided latitude, presumably, to do this yourself.

The first thing that comes to mind is the remarkable fact that no one, not the impressed reporter nor anyone in reply, thought there was anything inappropriate about the politician's exercise in Catholic criticism, and from a non-Catholic pulpit no less. It should have seemed too whimsical in a man who advocates the separation of Church and State and the inhibitions which he insists that separation imposes on his assertion

of many religious convictions in the public forum. The generous front-page attention his remarks received is no indication
of what kind of reception might be given in the unlikely event
of a non-Catholic celebrity criticizing his denomination from
a Catholic pulpit; and this only amplifies the voice of the
historian who called anti-Catholicism the anti-Semitism of the
liberals.

Secondly, one has to be struck by this official's own profession of theological influences on his executive policies. In fact
he named one: Teilhard de Chardin. There was a ring here
familiar to the announcement by President Carter that his
social conscience had been largely influenced by Reinhold
Niebuhr. It remains a tribute to Mr. Carter's patience and
acumen, for Niebuhr is not easy reading. Teilhard is even
harder. But Niebuhr may present the humanitarian vision with
a better prospect than does Teilhard. For while Teilhard's
cosmology is obscure, his sociology is not obscure enough;
indeed, it is not easy to conceal, except possibly from those
munificent and kind politicians who take only the best from
their theologians, Teilhard's benign regard for the early stages
of the Fascist experience, his verbal assaults on the racial worth
of the Chinese, and his campaign against black African membership in the fledgling United Nations.

Since the public official in question would most certainly
not hold such views, he does complicate his politics with his
theological allusions so that one is almost encouraged to agree
that religion has no place in politics. But this usually means
only that the practice of religion has no place, for the religious
label is always given a welcome place when it is useful. A
prominent party official recently proposed a congresswoman
for an even higher public office saying: "She's from New York,
she's a Catholic, she's been an effective [member of the House],
and she's very smart." In the 1984 primary campaign, the three

leading contenders were a man who advertised himself as the son of a preacher, a former Protestant divinity student, and an ordained Protestant clergyman whose speeches were nothing less than sermons. These are not out of place; they have a solid and good tradition behind them. But it is very much out of place to require of a Catholic candidate a mutability of doctrine and an infidelity to his or her obligatory commitments which would not be required of anyone else. Everyone should object to the Uncle Tom-ism by which Catholics running for office are expected to give a version of themselves which accords with the beliefs of the non-believer. It is even worse when Catholic politicians agree to this at the expense of docility to higher authority. In a general reference, Pope Leo XIII taught in the encyclical *Immortale Dei*, "...it is unlawful to follow one line of conduct in private and another in public, respecting privately the authority of the Church, but publicly rejecting it." So the national press applauded the Church for excommunicating several opponents of civil rights in Louisiana. To the point, a Catholic politician who finds it inexpedient to oppose pro-abortion legislation publicly must bear in mind the explicit counsel of the Sacred Congregation for the Doctrine of the Faith:

> Human law can abstain from punishment, but it cannot declare to be right what would be opposed to the natural law, for this opposition suffices to give the assurance that the law is not a law at all. It must in any case be clearly understood that whatever may be laid down by civil law in this matter, man can never obey a law which is in itself immoral, and such is the case of a law which would admit in principle the liceity of abortion. Nor can he take part in a propaganda campaign in favor of such a law, or vote for it. Moreover, he may not collaborate in its application.
>
> (Declaration on Procured Abortion, November 18, 1974)

Should this appear to promote "single-issue" voting, the Bishops of the New York State Catholic Conference explained in 1982 that "in the final analysis an overwhelming number of people vote for candidates because of 'single issues', even such single issues as a candidate's appearing to be a hawk or a dove.... Yet voters who express grave concern that four thousand unborn children are put to death through abortion every single day in the United States are apparently expected to remain silent in our 'pluralistic culture'...." Moreover, abortion is not so much a single issue as it is a total issue, a focus of the confrontation between secular materialism and supernatural humanism which is now having its effective test in the polling places of America.

The Obligation to Sanctity

Moral lassitude in public life at this decisive moment may be less a surrender to secularity than a surrender to the illogic of secularity. For secularity sees nothing rapacious in appropriating the universal language of the virtues for selective moral expression, even to the extent of calling a political opponent a bad Christian. The clearest life-and-death example of this is the readiness with which a legislator may oppose capital punishment, and sometimes even nuclear deterrence, on the ethical ground which he or she will not extend to protecting the lives of the unborn.

Writing in the *Human Life Review* (Winter 1984), Mary Meehan documented some telling instances of this. Former congresswoman Bella Abzug said in 1977 that she opposed the death penalty because "it's against my religious tradition" and thus she managed not only to transgress that reticence between private religious opinion and public conscience which she has been known to commend, but also to misrepresent her religion. The case is no less sanguine with some Catholic political figures. Governor Hugh Carey addressed the same issue of capital punishment saying, "I must respond to those very personal judgments that I hold and that I cannot discard by virtue of my office." And Senator Kennedy, another eager advocate of abortion funding, appealed for clemency toward the assassin of his brother Robert with a plea that "the kind of man my brother was . . . should be weighed in the balance on the side of compassion, mercy, and God's gift of life itself."

A Catholic should not enter public life unless willing to look on such office the way any Catholic should look on any job, as a means of becoming a saint. Sanctification in daily life is an obligation and not an option. To avoid temptations to lukewarmness and mendacity along the way, every Catholic in the public eye should have a spiritual director who is sound enough to represent only what accords with Catholic truth and who is detached enough not to be tailored in the livery of a courtier or flatterer but to speak when necessary as Nathan did to David: "Thou art the man" (2 Sam 12:7).

Fortitude may be the virtue rarest among public figures. Intelligence and zeal are no substitutes for it. It is a supernatural virtue, related to magnanimity, patience, munificence, and constancy, without which public administration is a threat to the common good. St. Thomas Aquinas analyzes fortitude, in language not irrelevant to politics, as he describes its double object: one is the repression of that fear which compromises an individual who desires to do good but who knows the possible negative consequences; the other consists in control of that bravado which, if unchecked, easily lapses into temerity when tested by competition (S. Th. IIa IIae, q.123, a.3). Fortitude then requires a capacity for suffering, not in the lesser sense of compassion which is known by the intelligentsia as "sensitivity", but in the mystagogic sense of that word as Christ displayed it: "suffering with". Pilate's irresponsibility lay in his contempt for his constituents, a disdain which accorded them the choice to inflict suffering on themselves. So long as the crowd was willing to say, "Let this crime be on us and on our children", he was willing to be pro-choice. Reluctant from the cynical perspective of the Latin imperium to muddle his civil religion with any profounder ontology, he washed his hands; but in such circumstances pale hands are a whitened euphemism for conscience.

Christian history bulges with examples of Catholic leaders who flouted Catholic teaching before cheering crowds, but the modern situation is unique in its cases of individuals who parade devout obedience to a Catholicism of their own definition. And then, for instance, when the Holy See refuses to approve inaccurate representations of Catholic teaching, removing the *Imprimatur* from unsuitable catechetical books, some Catholics themselves look upon it as an attack on the Constitutional principle of freedom of the press instead of recognizing in it a resolution of Catholic identity. When an archbishop challenges a municipal executive order which condones disordered sexual activity, some of his own flock act embarrassed at finding themselves members of an institution which contradicts the mayor.

While some notorious tyrannies claimed nominal Catholic identity, they were aberrations of the Catholic social economy. That is why bad Catholics were usually condemned, not for their Catholicity, but for their hypocrisy. But with the fragmentation of the Catholic world view, there came on the scene something more menacing than those quixotic and eccentric despotisms, and that was the modern invention called totalitarianism. Now totalitarianism is what we have when a social order based on natural law is rejected, not as a concession to pride, but as a matter of pride elevated to a high principle. It is a new product of the umbrous mental occlusion introduced by that rationalism which thought it was a form of enlightenment, but which can be traced over a tortuous path, as we allowed earlier, to the first formulations of individualism in the Reformation.

With this awareness, and using language which runs against the fashion of the moment and which may have to be whispered in classrooms, G. K. Chesterton, in his life of Aquinas, called Martin Luther the "elemental barbarian". At a time when we are occupied with George Orwell's appropriation of the year 1984, it is well to recall that the more courageous humanism of Chesterton also had its play in 1984, although no one seems to have remarked the coincidence, for that was also the date of his *Napoleon of Notting Hill,* exalting the perdurability of the good. But Chesterton's confidence also knew the darkness of human rebellion against the Authority which wills the human good. He traced the development this way: in Luther the force of a single personality, or what a public figure today might call "charisma", first claimed a worth equal to, and indeed superior to, the systematic logic of natural law and the life of the virtues.

As that distortion of personality has increased, the worthy democratic dictum, "every man a king", has been vulgarized into the modern conceit which insists "every man a kingdom". Louis XIV said, with perfect justice when you realize he was Louis XIV, *"L'état, c'est moi."* The energetic barbarian, envisioned by J. S. Mill, like the elemental barbarian remembered by Chesterton, says with no warrant, *"Je suis mon état."* And, according to the life of the virtues, that bravado soon succumbs to a spirit of temerity the moment reality intrudes far enough to show that egoism is still not the conscience of the universe. Here is rooted that Twentieth Century plague called

Alienation which has ruined more people than the Black Death of a dimmer age.

An Anthropological Fact

As Christians are coming to realize after at least eighty-four years spent trying to adapt Christianity to the Twentieth Century, the Twenty-First Century is closer to us than most of this present one. If Catholics are to save the next generations from the many mistakes of recent ones, they will be obliged to outlive modernity with its wholesale rejection of objectivity. For one monument of intellect stands out so large and clear that it is less noticeable than it would be were it smaller and duller, and it is this: the social disasters of the modern age, and the irresponsibility of public leaders in handling them, have been caused by the rejection of basic Catholic anthropology.

The conscience of the public Catholic once again needs to embrace the Catholic conception of morality as a dimension of the human condition, not extrinsically imposed but intrinsic to things human. The covenant between God and the Hebrew tribes was no contract accepting certain arbitrary rules; it was an agreement to obey that which can only be disobeyed at the price of self-destruction. Sin is de-humanizing, while virtue secures the human integrity. But neither is the moral standard separable from God, for it is necessary to the economy provided by him; and therefore it is objective and neither a projection of human theory nor an altruistic convention. It is intrinsic to freedom, assuring the development of the personality according to the proper human character, the responsible living out of the vocation which God has given to man, the antidote to alienation and cultural amnesia in all its forms. So the divine economy consists in universal norms which are not predilections which we can willfully choose or reject while remaining secure in our humanity.

To prevent the slavery of disordered inclinations to sensuality, restrictions have to be imposed by society, and these constitute what Aquinas called the *lex fomitis*. But our ethical nature is deeper than legislated inhibitions and permissions. Consequently, the civil law, as it is related to the moral realities, does not exempt anyone from the conscience's obligations to the natural law. Catholic politicians cannot ethically cite personal opposition to injustice as an excuse for not opposing it in public. The fact of conscience requires that they publish their moral opposition to it, and promote access only to what serves the human character as it is willed by God.

The Catholic politician speaks from a tradition which transfigures civilization by the light of culture. It is a light which is ordained by the divine will to give light to the whole house. The light shines on the just and on the unjust alike, and justice is the acceptance of the fact. The practice of justice, then, is the institutionalization of reality. In the framework of this institution, no one has the right to impose one's sense of human integrity on anyone else, but every just man according to justice has the solemn duty to impose it on himself. And when it is also God's sense of morality, he has a vocation to promote it by just law on the whole social order. Then the real world, which by all accounts includes the *New York Times,* will understand that no one is a victim of innocence. The innocent are victims of that disordered mentality which will not vindicate innocence.

V

PIETY AND LEARNING

God and Our Ancestors

At a benefit dinner in the ballroom of a New York hotel, a young fellow in evening clothes expressed to me his admiration for Adam Smith as a great Catholic leader. During the course of his remarks it became clear that he, not a Catholic himself, meant the late Governor Al Smith, for whom I have expressed admiration on other occasions. There was no purpose in listing the differences between the two Smiths; and it would have been rude to remark the ignorance of one who advertised himself as having been well and expensively educated. He was not unrecollected or absentminded; his was not a slip of the tongue; he was genuinely surprised to know that Adam Smith was not Al Smith. The problem was this, it seemed to me: if he had been able to distinguish the differences between the two, he would probably have remained at a disadvantage to describe the similarities between them. And it is important that everyone be able to acknowledge at least one special quality they shared, one thing which should be common to civilized people, one instinctive gift by which people become vernacular inhabitants of a long culture. That of which I speak, the possession of those in different stations of life and treasured by worthy men and women rich and poor, is Pietas.

By remaining oblivious to its wonders, the young man with eager expression above his starched shirt was a kind and unwitting barbarian. I do not use the word lightly; nor do I altogether blame him. And the chief victim of his domesticated barbarity was himself, who may live a life in partial dimensions for not having enjoyed the reverence of so fine a gift. Piety, classically, is duty to the gods and to the ancestors. The concepts of dignity, freedom, industry, and patriotism flow through this sense of double obligation. The two Smiths, so unlike each other in countless ways, belonged to the same fraternity of piety, both aware of the attentions proper to the ultimate principles in creation, and to perfect eternal happiness. The double classical construction is a delicate and necessary balance: order and happiness. Universals are the reference for human bliss. The Psalmist asks universally: "When I survey the heavens, the moon and the stars which thou hast ordained, what is man that thou art mindful of him . . . ", and then he adds particularly: " . . . and the son of man that thou visitest him?" (Ps 8:3–4). Impiety is fruitless because it rejects the association between universal order and happiness. We might say without exaggeration that it is the definitive barbarism; no civilization, pagan or Christian, has been impious in its endeavors, no matter how poorly it performed its civilized duties. It was true to the Greek and to the Hebrew. So Aristotle writes in *On the Parts of Animals:*

> Having already treated of the celestial world, as far as our conjectures could reach, we proceed to treat of animals, without omitting, to the best of our ability, any member of the kingdom, however ignoble. For if some have no graces to charm the sense, yet even these, by disclosing to intellectual perception the artistic spirit that designed them, give immense pleasure to all who can trace links of causation, and are inclined to philosophy.

A philosophy lurks behind the paleontology, as it did when Hamlet held up the skull of Yorick long before Dr. Leakey examined the skull of Pithecanthropus. The man in the cave may have had his own jests, yet unaided physical science is impervious to them. The handicap of scientific analysis lies precisely in that: it does not discern the person in the person. It has useful means of knowing certain things clearly, but it cannot know them "well" as did the Danish prince, and the Greek wise man, and the Hebrew harpist. It is not a moral deficiency; the proper end of physical science is not in such information. The paleontologist digs up, the philosopher digs down; and the difference is as palpable as an airplane landing and an aviator landing.

But this pretty obvious fact can only be appreciated by rejecting the mistake of thinking that knowledge is inevitably progressive, or that we know better by knowing more. If the intellect does not discern the qualitative difference, the information it has will alienate the informed from the object of the knowledge. How is it, for instance, that a philosopher-playwright can possibly have a wider, if not more schematic, sense of the human condition than a man who dates human bones and puts them back together again? And how is it that Adam Smith and Al Smith were both more sophisticated than the Young Modern who confused them?

Were one not to ask, I should still answer this: they were pious. It is the background of the whole educating curriculum, even when we disagree about its implications or how we should go about it. I do not expect that either Smith would have thought the other a paragon of piety; neither thought of himself in such terms most of the time. It was not characteristic of them that they spelled these things out. But when Pope John Paul II says that "prophecy requires memory", there is no doubt that they would have known what he meant and would have agreed, though the memories were not the same. Deep perception requires a knowledge of sources; I do not think the

Pope put that more elliptically than the elderly mother of a
famous writer, who remarked of herself in a mirror, "Isn't it
amazing that anyone so old can be so beautiful?" The piety can
be located somewhere between the mother saying it and the
son remembering it.

In the prophetic idiom, all intelligent activity is of a piece
with the piety which gives perspective to what is knowable. If
someone chooses to limit his information to what is available
on the computer screen, the rapture of looking into a mirror
and seeing the universe there will be beyond comprehension.
Hume went so far as to say that anyone who inquired of the
whys and wherefores of such available genius "would throw
himself into a chimera". But the subtleties of commingling the
creative intellect and the contemplative intellect become apparent the more thought is of both the world and the God behind
the world.

Education is a function of all the spiritual gifts of the intellect,
the first of which is wisdom; and piety defines their posture.
As a duty to the divine, it situates the intellective faculty in a
transcendent universal reference; as a duty to its own precedents,
it finds a relationship for the individual in the part of that
order which is human. As cosmology is a consistent commentary on the universe, so piety is the ground of that commentary's
moral application. Without it, education is little other than a
materialist didacticism, capable of reducing universals to pantheism or atheism (the very possibility of the two as alterna-
tives cancelling each), and reducing singularities of experience
to the illusion of solipsism; and of course, solipsism is contradicted
immediately when solipsists try to proselytize.

But piety, unaided by metaphysical revelation of truth, can
produce these errors itself. If the analogy between the gods and
the creatures of the gods does not admit of the true God, and if
the ancestral idiom lacks the model of the saints, then the most

one might hope for is Aristotle's kind of verdant natural theology. At this great moment of scientific discovery, learning can be *buccinator novi temporis,* not by the remoteness of Buddha on his pillow, nor the materialism of Comte in his bureau, nor the quasi-mysticism of natural religion without metaphysical exactions; it will happen by recovering the Catholic refinements which understand the implications of man in the image of God. If the failure of Western pragmatism is in its lack of place for ontology in the universal system, such as was Francis Bacon's neglect, philosophy and theology can be reordered without confusion by the Catholic sacramental wisdom which gives right direction to the pious mind.

Dignum et Justum Est

"What is man that thou art mindful of him?" The mindfulness of the mind can remain a melancholy apostrophe, as it has in all the world's tragedies and languid romances. If asked outside the Catholic tradition of universals and particulars, it will keep sounding in modern mental chambers, as if we were designed to do nothing but circle in a sphere-less universe. Christopher Dawson proposes this cogency in his essay, "A Universal Spiritual Society": "Two essential characteristics distinguish the Christian faith and the Catholic Church: uniqueness and universality." There is a hymn possibly surpassing all others in witness, and it lies at the heart of the central act of Catholic life; this is the *Sursum Corda* of the Holy Eucharist. In this moment of human preparation for divine encounter, the priest bids the didactic and synagogic speech of the first part of the Liturgy to yield in tribute to transcendent discourse. Reason is not abandoned, as it would be in sensate systems; rather, it attains its full place in the analogy of being. The respective orders of existence, unique in themselves in terms of angelic choirs and saintly ranks, join the human assembly in adoration of the one divine Essence: "Lift up your hearts./We lift them up to the Lord./Let us give thanks to the Lord our God./It is right to give him thanks and praise." Then, after the definition of the celebrated mystery, in a chorus of angels and men: "Holy, Holy, Holy Lord,/God of power and might./Heaven and earth are full of your glory./ Hosanna in the highest./Blessed is he who comes in the name of the Lord./Hosanna in the highest."

The rational qualification for this is the necessity of pious duty: *"Dignum et justum est"*, the Church's decisive response, which is weakly translated "It is right. . . . " The categories are those of ontology (it is worthy of fact) and morality (it is suitable to the proper end). When these two standards are not appreciated or used as governing principles for determining acts, the dignity of created design is fragmented into a sectarian view of the world; and the concept of rightful purpose is rejected for a secular humanism which operates according to simplistic efficiency. In the vernacular of Western democracies, sectarianism and secularism have taken the shape of pluralism and liberalism, each in some measure an aberration of the analogy of being. There have been figures in the modern age who saw the problem and sought to establish a better order according to the Catholic vision of dignity and justice: Adenauer, de Gasperi, and De Gaulle. But few supported or even understood their highest aim.

The social historian can point out the effect that the failure of democracy to realize the Catholic social vision has had directly on education. In the United States, for instance, the dominant academic model has been Calvinist. The Catholic concept of a suitably ordered placement of individuals in a universal scheme has been obscured, and part of the reason is the general social disregard for the Christian saints as the operative model for enlightened existence. Dawson himself recognized the irony of placing learning in the line of Protestant rather than Catholic culture. Contrary to received clichés, the Reformation spirit is not prophetic but primarily didactic for being an incomplete account of the relationship between ontological and cosmological discourse. The prophetic experience is proper to Catholicism for being an intellectualization of the tradition of culture. As Protestant voluntarism moved to a more lethargic kind of liberal materialism in industrial society, this dichotomy became more glaring. By its duties, piety is the moral vehicle for prophetic discourse; in the Protestant experience it largely became an uncoordinated pietism which disengaged learning from a universal system.

At the present stage of intellectual decomposition in the Western societies, what should be obvious has to be stated as though it were a startling and controversial idea: the right idea of a university—and of its contingent enterprises—requires a right concept of the universe. From this there follows an even more specific point of contention, but without it our academies will turn out space engineers and astronauts incapable of an idyll more profound than nursery rhymes about twinkling little stars: the right idea of knowledge and learning in the university also has to be the right idea of individuation and universal truth.

A system of education respects the principle of individuation by teaching the arts of leadership and moral responsibility, as functions of charismatic individuality. But it is neglectful of its purpose if it does not also teach how to obey leadership, in deference to the universally ordered hierarchy of truths. Here one can compliment the college which, it is said, accepted a student who described herself as a follower, on the grounds that every other freshman considered herself a leader and would therefore appreciate having someone to lead. But it is also true that a mark of modern society has been the dearth of suitable leaders of stature; and this should not be surprising, if the schools have not inspired learners with a large vision of the world in which they are being formed. Once again, the problem is referred to a lack of piety. A mechanistic social responsibility is not inspiring enough to build character; greatness is very much born of knowing that your duty is to heaven and the honor of the past.

The Prophetic Light

Even the original Reformation sensibilities of learning referred to the Talmudic and Scholastic concept of piety as duty; and they employed it with remarkable success to awaken the emerging American nation to its cultural potential. There is the venerable song about the founder of a colonial college: "Eleazar Wheelock was a very pious man/He went into the wilderness to teach the Indian." The song has been suppressed by the college's officials because a select committee decided that it denigrates the Indian. Inasmuch as the clergyman is said in the song to have introduced a curriculum consisting entirely of five hundred gallons of New England rum, it should be more offensive to the Puritans. But few of them exist anymore; or, having puritanized the savages, they have nothing left to do but savage themselves. The college seal remains unscathed, however, a splendid example of primitive art; and primitivism is a far nobler thing than savagery and a far more elegant thing than puritanism. The picture on it shows a shaft of sharp light illuminating a path before two naked Indians who are holding a large Bible which they are about to devour one way or another. For all the rantings of the determinists, and for all the ravings of the social Darwinists, the picture is of a high and subtle excellence: it could hardly portray any better the ambiguous stance of the modern American undergraduate in the presence of prophetic knowledge. To a higher degree, it is symbolic of something unfamiliar to both colonial clergymen and modern students: the description of prophetic light according to St. Thomas Aquinas.

St. Thomas numbered four kinds of light (II.IIae, q.17, art.2). First, sensory light, perceived by the organic sense of humans and the higher animals alike. Second, intelligible light, which is human intelligence as the power of insight and understanding, commonly acknowledged by a universal philosophical tradition since Socrates until it was scrambled by Locke and Hume. To skip for a moment, the fourth and most exalted light is the vision of divinity; and the privilege of it is reserved for the blessed ones in heaven. But the third, which I am talking about now, is the prophetic light; this is the illumination which showers rays on all humans in their original sensory nakedness. By means of the third light, the sensory faculties have their association with the divine. It is not an element of organic experience, but of knowledge. And its corporeal evidence is in human discourse, a deliberately chosen word since a discourse advances by successive steps, subject to error, and opposed to an "intuitive" knowledge of which only pure spirits, the holy angels, are perfectly capable.

The piety operative in a Catholic economy is responsible to all four kinds of light. The first light is primarily domestic: sensory perception is native to the womb and cradle, preceding any institutionalized structuralism. And an education is incomplete which does not extend beyond the second light of unassisted human intelligence. By ignoring this glaring fact, modern pedagogues did incalculable harm to the mental welfare of several generations. As society has learned by a bitter experience of the recent decades, an individual left at the second stage of illumination is not properly articulate or wise, and easily reverts to the primary level of exclusive sensory perception. One need only look at the consumerist and sybaritic complexes of the post-war generations for a psychedelic picture of what that implies.

By fostering this servile mentality, the modern university betrayed its very purpose in the commonweal. How this happened is beyond the scope of any single essay such as this; but it certainly could not have happened without a gullibility for the three contradictions of piety: the will to power, the tyranny of the subconscious, and economic dialecticism. Each offers on its own terms the exploitation of the created order as the only relief for the social dislocation within that order. In one way or another they are reflected in the simple pragmatism of a democratic culture which claims to be free of all three. How else, for instance, can one explain the growing tendency to turn higher education into occupational training? It is more than well that applied sciences flourish; but the culture served by technology is jeopardized when, as in the United States between 1963 and 1983, the number of degrees granted in the fields of technical sciences and crafts more than doubled, and business degrees increased eighty-seven percent, while there was a fifty-eight percent decline in foreign language study, a drop of sixty percent in philosophy, and seventy-two percent in English. By 1984 the majority of university graduates had no foreign language, 75 percent had studied no European history, and 86 percent were innocent of any familiarity with classical civilization. The moment a student evaluates an academic subject by what he has come to call its "usefulness", he has become a slave of the exploitive process: blind to intelligibility, deaf to prophecy, and crippled in the ancestral procession.

But an order is still at work where the responsibilities of culture obtain, and it provides, by a delicate kind of syllogism, the pattern of the liberal arts according to the Catholic vision. It is this: the mission of a school is the dissemination of knowledge; the mission of Catholicism is the salvation of the human race; the mission of the Catholic school is to teach the human race the way to salvation by means of knowledge disseminated in a suitable and just way. *"Dignum et justum est."* By such display, the school takes its proper place in the eucharistic dialogue of creation. No school does this just by offering "courses" in Catholic doctrine as a gloss on scientific principles, or by providing Catholic chaplains as ancillary to academic life. The Catholic synthesis means first that the concept of mission in education be given priority over function: for the suitability of anything is measured more by its aptness to its purpose than by its conformity to temporary predilections. It does not serve any vital purpose to ask if a subject taught is useful if the idea of usefulness is not properly understood. And if a school does not teach the philosophy of usefulness, it is of little use itself, and can only expect to hatch little utilitarians. The right understanding is to be had through the liberal arts, and while there is a tradition of the liberal arts outside Catholic culture, the arts properly attain their integrity within the same scheme upon which all dutiful life should be intent; knowledge, in other words, is of incomplete service, and becomes very much of a disservice, until it helps the knower to attain his moral status in the order of the universal reality. The term for that status, as it is *dignum et justum* to the human condition, is salvation.

The Unifying Principle

I do not mean from the above that teaching is exclusively a form of credal proselytizing, although it must invariably proselytize for something that is thought to be true, or there would be no need to teach; nor do I mean that a Catholic education is not Catholic if it does not secure the internal assent of conscience. Such would deny the objective value of the university as the institutionalization of inquiry. Were the case any other, conscience would not hold the primacy of place which it irrefutably enjoys in Catholic thought. It is a Scholastic tenet that the denigration of the creature denigrates the Creator. But as a necessary corollary, reason has to be integrated with a systematic and transcendent trust, if it is not to become that ingredient of servility which is rationalism. Rationalism prevents inquiry from attaining universal truth. The Catholic university is obliged to refute it by the scientific logic which holds truth to be true; and as Catholicism is held to be true, so it should be taught as true in a Catholic university. Those who decide that this compromises their freedom of inquiry, have no responsibility to teach what they want there; they do have a moral obligation to teach it elsewhere. A true form of reason obtains where there is no rationalizing, and the authority of reason in sacred tradition forms the conscience so that it does not become the tyrant it is when left alone:

> For the wrath of God is revealed from heaven against all ungodliness and wickedness of men who by their wickedness suppress the truth. For what can be known about God is plain to them, because God has shown it to them. Ever since the creation of the world his invisible nature, namely, his eternal power and deity, has been clearly perceived in the things that have been made. So they are without excuse; for although they knew God they did not honor him as God or give thanks to him, but they became

futile in their thinking and their senseless minds were darkened.
Claiming to be wise, they became fools, and exchanged the
glory of the immortal God for images resembling mortal man
or birds or animals or reptiles (Rom 1:18–23).

This obligation of reason to a higher authority commonly
seems to deny reason in the estimation of the naturalist. George
Bernard Shaw certainly did not understand it; so to his way of
thinking, which he thought was a very high way of thinking,
a Catholic university is a contradiction in terms. But his way of
thinking, if consistent, would have called a Ford automobile a
contradiction in terms. Any rational thinker can say with far
more reason that an Atheist university is a contradiction in
terms: the ability to deny God is a lax use of a gift of God. And
an Agnostic university is an improvement only in the sense
that a disease like laryngitis can be said to have improved when
it has been arrested. The ability not to know God is an exercise
in absentmindedness on the grandest of scales, a kind of cosmic
donnishness which ignores the Creator as a habit of its own
lack of creativity. In a secular society with plural values, the
university has an even greater obligation; for pluralism as the
naturalist ordinarily means it denies the coherence of meaning.
Culture then turns to the university for the rational synthesis
needed to sustain the healthy society. A Catholic university
which secularizes itself becomes part of the social problem.

Reason and faith are different in the way of complements;
they are mutually necessary in the pursuit of wisdom precisely
because of the difference between them. Left apart, the one
staggers through a maze of rationalism which appears straight
only when you stop short of a corner; the other drifts through
a mist of pietistic voluntarism which provides a safe path only
when you do not move. The excited revulsion of the Thomists
against the Averroists seems totally extravagant to modern

opinion, but the Thomists rightly understood the dangers of compartmentalizing "science" and "religion" as though they should be strangers to each other. The Averroist philosophy makes enough sense if you begin with the false premise of tension between reason and faith: Dante even placed the chief culprit, Siger of Brabant, among the Doctors of the Church. But left to its own devices, Averroism would have hastened the schizophrenic approach to empiricism and intuition which the Protestant split unloosed with its many sad consequences.

The Catholic and the classical pagan have enjoyed an affinity which made them closer to each other than either has been to the rationalist and the pietist: their common acceptance of pious duty, if only a kind of culturism in the case of many of the pagans, sought the knowledge of the universal principles of creation and the particular attainment of perfect happiness. Before the coming of Christianity, the noblest sign of science was Caduceus, the snaky wand held by Hermes Trismegistus: one serpent Knowledge, and the other Wisdom. It was the pagan equivalent of the type of Moses' staff in the wilderness. Crucified Christ united the two capacities of intelligence: the crucifix belongs on the wall of the classroom as properly as on the wall of the church, for it is the sublime historicization of the old mythic longing for the resolution of truths and Truth.

The Christian vision cannot be blind to naturalist perception where it has been rational and humane. Christianity has rather made the university a kind of Cana, the little schoolroom of Calvary, where the primitive water of mythical assignation is turned into the wine of historical revelation. The liberal arts are basically the culturation of that process, though it is a difficult one and quite capable of, shall we say, drunken excess. I refer specifically to the Renaissance eclectics. Then it was a degeneration masked as regeneration. But the classical tradition would be unknown today, had it not been for the recovery of it by Catholic culture. The derogatory term "Gothic" was in fact an emotional plea for things classical by the Catholic stalwarts. As pure aestheticism, of course, the classical motif becomes the artificial melody of deism. Enriched by a higher sacramental wisdom, however, it fulfills its own beautiful longing. The great pagan moralist Seneca, to whom is attributed some apocryphal correspondence with St. Paul, wrote from a profound natural piety: *"Habui enim illos tamquam amissurus."* The nobility of it, esteeming others as one about to lose them, is only increased by the knowledge of a resurrection. The lapidary inscription for Cardinal di Poggia near the Church of Santa Sabina turns Seneca's crystalline water into a richer vintage, at no cost to high Latinity: *"Ut moriens viveret vixit ut moriturus."* A whole science of theology might be drawn from a comparison of these future participles; the Cardinal "lived as one about to die", but for a reason puzzling to the Stoic: "so that dying he might live". Through the fraternity of piety, the grammar of the Roman Stoic becomes the grammar of the Roman Catholic.

Alma Mater

Nothing is lost to culture in overwhelming the pagan sense of loss; but much is lost in attempts to overwhelm what Christianity has found. Pagan piety was antecedent to Christian piety, and was not invented to contradict it. But modern secularity is an outright denial of the metaphysics which has given substance to the maturation of piety: it portrays man as an evolutionary product of nature incapable of survival after death, and takes for granted the futility of moral solutions outside the scope of scientific method. But, given the order of intelligibility, that kind of modern prejudice is to wisdom what narcissism is to sexuality, what greed is to consumption, and what egoism is to romance. It fractures human perception by denying the universal duty to God and to the epistemological tradition. One could say secularism is a philosophical form of amnesia. And as "prophecy requires memory", the loss of piety is more catastrophic than the Stoic loss of a friend; it is the loss of all cultural antecedents. Of course the documents and edifices of the ages remain in various states of preservation; but the people who have forgotten their human duties to them may peruse them and crawl over them like chattering animals in a rain forest, poking and sniffing at some artifact of civilization left behind by explorers. I do not think this is an exaggeration. Graffiti are an adolescent version of it, but every sack of a city has shown that adults are capable of it. And in each case, the vandals have instinctively marched upon the university in the city.

The habit is as unspeakable and final as matricide, and in the order of things it is the same: a school is called Alma Mater, not obliquely but by a sharp intuition deeper than sentiment. The occupants of chairs of teaching represent the maternal function of guarding tribal memory. The figure of Alma Mater cannot adequately be an anonymous statue in front of the college library; the functional piety of memory is represented by the Pietà, the Lady holding eternal Wisdom on her lap. The model seems to have first appeared early in the thirteenth century, just at the time that the concept of the university appeared. Wisdom is scarred by human ignorance, and voluntarily bears the wounds of original pride. As testimony to the drama of wisdom, the Pieta is also the record of history: the Alma Mater of the intellect once nursed ancient Wisdom when he appeared to wise men as an infant in the company of animals; and she sought him sorrowing until she collected him back to herself when he was twelve years old and an enigma to the *savants* in the Temple. The highest science of any curriculum consists in discerning how one young woman united duty to her God and duty to her tribe so perfectly that she, untutored by any master save humility, became the ageless Seat of Wisdom.

The Duty of Conscience

To say the least, the imagery of the Lady and Wisdom is an anxious proposition to the secularist. But the Second Vatican Council, in its Declaration on Catholic Education (n.10), located the true ground of intellectual freedom in this pious economy. Liberty for scientific inquiry is best secured in the light of prophetic revelation. Appeal to academic freedom is untenable if it rejects the memory of universal principles and the commitment to humility. By way of corollary, a professor should be attached to a reference loftier than academic tenure for the proper exercise of academic freedom. The human duty to the perduring wisdom of culture means that scientific inquiry is not arbitrary inquiry: research is intended for a conclusion. The sort of secular figure who does not understand this is the secularist who has made the fact of secular reality a religious principle, a secularism; it is not unlike the deist's mistake of making the fact of deity a religion of itself, a deism, in which the religion of God became God-as-religion. To secularize the world is like deifying God; it is a remarkably clumsy insult to the object being honored. What is left is an idol, and the fabricator alienates himself from the real thing. Secularism is no more worldly-wise than deism is mystical. The secularist does not understand the nature of right conclusions about the world. So he uses conscience as an excuse for bias and not as a guide to responsible decisions. Conscience determines the propriety of inquiry ordered to its end, which must be truth. And we declare a principle which has guided every legitimate scholarly pursuit when we say that the conscience, to be freely human, conforms to the divine will. In an expression of St. Thomas (*De veritate,* q.17, a.4, ad.2), conscience is "the coming of divine precept to man".

Academic enterprise cannot justify dissent from the Church's definitions of the divine will, and still be consistent about the necessary constituents of freedom. That would not be empiricism but blind faith, for trust in anything apart from its justifying authority is credulity; and the Church lives as the bastion against that kind of egoism in an increasingly credulous world.

Not the Second, but the First, Vatican Council initiated a complaint against uninformed belief. It was talking about liberal materialism, which it refuted by citing the Letter to the Romans (12:1) to explain the obedience of faith to reason. But the reason, to be rational, is dutiful to the operation of supernatural grace lest, in the words of Karl Adam, the scholar succumb to "self-sufficient and isolated thinking" and pursue an "eccentric subjectivism".

What passes for learning today in many, if not most, sinecures of the Western academic establishment, is exactly such eccentricity. The idolatry of the secularized intelligence is an arid form of anthropomorphism, recasting immutable universals in the molds of mutable conceit. When contemptuous of its duty to historical fact and the universal culture of experience, the university dismisses the patrimony of tradition as though it were an archaism, promotes compulsory social controls and populations engineered according to its private designs, and defends a moral code which has been the source of every social collapse in the history of human affairs. And each assault on reason is enforced in the name of reason. This is the troublesome thing: the method is sceptical rather than rational, and scepticism as a dogmatic principle is self-destructive. The de-population of the schools as a consequence of reduced fertility rates bears mute witness to the ravages of a culture's self-cannibalization; vacancy signs on the campuses silently indict the vacant minds which thought there were too many people.

An unexpected source, the Brookings Institution, has published the result of three years of study, *Religion in American Public Life,* which flatly asserts that secularism is no sound basis for a democratic society. It says this with a clarity which popular intimidation has removed from the texts of self-conscious Christian intellectuals: "Human rights are rooted in the moral worth with which a loving Creator has endowed each human soul, and social authority is legitimized by making it answerable to transcendent moral law."

The basic human right is the right to life; and the intellect forsakes empirical responsibility to that right the more it becomes sceptical of the plausibility of souls. The Inquisitor was unenlightened when he destroyed bodies to save souls; it is far more dismal to destroy bodies that are thought to lack souls. In 1920, two professors published a book entitled *Die Freigabe der Vernichtung lebensunwerten Lebens,* "The Permission to Destroy Life Unworthy of Life". One, Karl Binding, had taught law at the University of Leipzig for forty years; Alfred Hoche was professor of psychiatry at the University of Freiburg. They spoke of the defenseless, crippled, and insane as "human ballast" and said that to kill them was "an allowable, useful act". It was but one book written by men remote in the world of academe; but the Nazis found the book, and soon university scientists and virtually the entire German medical profession allowed mock nurseries and asylums to become killing chambers.

In 1985, in a makeshift operating room attached to a Barcelona convention hall, abortions were performed on two mothers; the dead infants considered "unworthy of life" were placed in glass jars and carried into the hall as three thousand radical feminists applauded the spectacle. This was not Galicia of Caligula; it was modern Spain which had become infected by a cerebral contempt for the tradition of life. The date was sixty-five years after the publication of *lebensunwertes Lebens* theory. It was also the twenty-fifth anniversary of the more aesthetic occasion at the Museum of Modern Art in New York, when a sophisticated crowd had applauded the self-destruction of the sculptor Tinguely's mass of metal; in Barcelona people were now taking the metal's place. Though it has been said that modernity rejected the concept of damnation, the case is quite more extraordinary: modernity made damnation a social policy and an art form.

As in Fascist Germany, the medical profession in the contemporary world, abandoning the Hippocratic oath, is cooperating with the degeneration. Einstein once warned not to expect intellectuals to defend the best interest of society in times of crisis. The Barcelona event was as improbable as the horrors of earlier impieties, and for that reason it has been almost totally ignored. The moral conscience malformed by modern scientism rejects unscientifically any evidence that contradicts its fragile hypotheses. The miracle of the sun at Fatima was the best documented miracle of the modern age, and it was greeted with embarrassment by a wide public for that reason. The worse the sin, and the greater the miracle, the less likely the chance that they will be understood for what they are. Logically, unless there is a reordering of intuitions, we might expect soon to see audiences in convention halls applauding the execution of the crippled and the aged. The outrageousness of the possibility makes it all the more probable. And, given the habits of the mind, it might first be staged in the halls of a university.

The Youth of Tradition

When students in such an environment become the traditionalists to some degree, and the professors the iconoclasts, the persistence of piety is at work in a cogent way. Tradition is proper to the young who are supposed to be rebels, because any culture is a social rebellion against incoherence. Tradition is old only because it has kept itself younger than other things. Information ages, but wisdom enters the world as a child, recalling the human race to the time of its infancy. The iconoclast is a reactionary; he does not build new things with the vigor of youth, he reacts against old things in the exasperation of his own fixation with age. He lives in a time warp, and he tries to make the world look straight by warping it and himself. The child playing with building blocks is the traditionalist and his game is a massive piety; the adult smashing the blocks is the impious reactionary; and when he is very reactionary, he will start smashing the child.

The child is instinctively ritualistic. It is wrong to think that rituals are ornaments added to life; they are the acts by which life is transmitted. Informality is an embellishment to natural form; it has to be learned, when formality is simply given. The child in his private rituals may bow down before false gods, but he will not think it odd to bow down. He has to be stopped from it by an adult. He may think that the dark in the closet is evil and that the reflection on the wall is an intelligent spirit; but he will not think that there is no evil, or that angels are impossible. He has to be given that misinformation by an adult. Ritual gives the young an automatic posture; they do not feel a need to invent experience, for they are too busy beholding it. The loss of ritual consciousness is an adult complex; by that I do not mean it is mature, only that it is not youthful. One sign of the loss of the ritual sense is the increased need to manipulate the rites of life to make them "more meaningful". Youth is happily free of that, and rightly feels patronized when liturgies and protocols are toned down to an adult's idea of youthful taste. Ancient rituals are the youngest things in the world, for they are as elastic as tradition itself. Human thought can imagine progress, but can only attain it through a sacred tradition. Without this pious intuition, progress becomes progressivism, a motion never quite in motion, a movement anywhere except somewhere. Having rejected the life of tradition, the progressivist loses the vitality of his goal and ends up nowhere.

At the moment, progressivism has become entrenched in the universities which have become the establishment of the anti-establishmentarians of the 1960s. The progressivism assumes a variety of names in this time capsule: "structuralism", "deconstructionism", "radical feminism". And still it operates against the purpose of the university by making it home to a totalitarian defensiveness and a fortress of reaction at war with the working world.

Tradition cannot be reactionary and still operate; certainly it cannot be totalitarian, as totalitarianism is the egoist's *pastiche* of universality, and tradition is the authentic transmission of universals. By reason of universal reference, a traditionalist can confidently say that civilization may be entering a whole new anthropological stage. Language so breathtaking is beyond the toleration of the progressivist who is content to react against aging by thinking that he has come of age. A new stage in tradition is not what coming of age is in progress. Man entering a new stage in civilization takes on new duties; man who has come of age frees himself of them. This is why the progressivist tends to be a libertine. Having made a totally subjective estimation of himself, he embarks on a flight from human nature. The modern libertine is then the ultimate reactionary, for the reaction is against himself. He is not ashamed of wrong sex because he is ashamed of sexuality. In the progressivist's lack of vision, the creative purpose of sexual union becomes a disease to be cured by a pill, and the unitative purpose of the union is reversed for the gratification of the self which becomes its own object. The libertine spirit has fairly been called sexual suicide.

The only remedy is the theocentric knowledge of creation, but that was precisely what false pietism rejected in its rebellion against Catholic universals. The reactionary spirit of progressivism has its roots in the reactionary spirit of anti-Catholicism. In *Les Trois Reformateurs,* Maritain recounts the psychology of impiety, and it is nothing that is not being repeated in our own day: "Few spectacles were more shameless than what carnal frenzy offered in Germany. Religious of both sexes, unbound by Luther, were only looking for opportunities to detach themselves from the Church, like gangrene from the body." The reaction against nature has now situated itself wherever the Catholic system of universals has been dismissed, and this certainly includes the universities. Socially the effects are more widespread than ever a Catharist or Reformer might have dreamed. To deny the denial of the flesh's disorder is to deny the flesh its ordered existence. No one can think straight when that is the case.

Impurity denies the capacity for truth. There is no beauty without purity, no truth without purity; no goodness without purity. No one is well educated who does not practice the purity of moral intention; and it is an aridity of the first order to learn anything without controlling the will and the appetites. A scholar is not much of one when he lacks prudence, temperance, and so forth; and he is a pedant without the higher virtues. To deny that is further to fragment the universal order of intelligence and substance, and to lose a youth which can stay forever young.

Where this is understood, the life of the virtues is valued as a school in itself. The scholar of moral rectitude will be better at his work for living the virtues; he can only be inferior by their neglect. Between the virtues and the liberal arts is a kind of cooperative order. I speak specifically of those arts which Martianus Capella arranged after Varro in the fifth century, and Alcuin later instituted. We might say that the cardinal virtues have their counterparts in the quadrivium: music and justice are both sciences of harmony; arithmetic and prudence are sciences of order; geometry and temperance are sciences of imagination; astronomy and fortitude are sciences of transcendence. And the theological virtues comport themselves with the fundamental trivium: grammar being to discourse what faith is to supernatural conversation; rhetoric being to grammar what hope is morally to faith; and dialectic providing a natural analogy of the heavenly discourse of love, just as love is the highest logic of creation. It is an arbitrary scheme, to be sure, but a fair reminder of the community between natural and spiritual sciences.

But modern pedagogy has proposed a freak kind of fiction: study as a technique separable from moral purpose, a little like a brain kept alive in a pan. A monstrosity in science fiction, it is truly grotesque in the universities: self-righteousness runs about wildly when it is severed from righteousness. Blake's "dark satanic mills" may not have been the factories of Birmingham and Manchester; he could have meant the halls of Oxford and Cambridge whose latest tenants were succumbing to the rationalist thrall. The Prince of Lies spins his loom in the mind before he moves into the mill, and he can make the academy a slum more foul than any alley.

The Affliction of Pietism

Then the real foe of the flesh, pietism, is also the foe of the mind. By it, subjectivism breeds with all its ills and becomes a plague of the ephemeral modern mood. When Kant reversed the functional relationship between mind and reality, raising appearance to the dignity of objects, he laid the shaky foundation for pietistic indulgence. Inevitably, it can only conclude in sentimentality, as it is found today among impulsive enthusiasts; or in despair, the great examplar of which is the representative mystic of the Reformation line, Kierkegaard. The modern age is the last gasp of frivolous subjectivism, and those who still hold to it are remarkable in the seriousness with which they repeat its maxims. Schools still are replete with educators who have been taught by the humanistic psychologist Carl Rogers: "When an activity *feels* as though it is worthwhile, it *is* worth doing."

The Roman liturgy has a genius for dissecting and transcending these tendencies; one could say that each Eucharistic prayer is a stone in an architecture of perception. It is not easy even for the Catholic to appreciate the tectonic quality of this language. In her closing prayer for the Thirtieth Sunday in Ordinary Time, the Church prays: *"Perficiant in nobis, Domine, quaesumus, tua sacramenta quod continent, ut, quae nunc specie gerimus, rerum veritate capiamus."* The Lord is asked to grant that his sacraments might bring to perfection in us what they contain, so that we might be capable of truly possessing what we perform in sign. It is a wonderful exposition of the objectivity of grace and the subjective response; with exquisite gracefulness, it declares the operation of habitual grace to be both *gratis data* and *gratum faciens,* a pure gift which grants holiness to those who receive it on its terms. The official English translation, as it now stands, misses the subtlety: "Lord, bring to perfection within us the communion we share in this sacrament. May our celebration have an effect in our lives." I hope it is not undue to say that this does not convey the original sacramental theology. I am not saying that it implies a wrong idea of justification, or anything like that; but it does understate, at least by diction, the objectivity of sanctifying grace: what Pius XI in his Encyclical *Casti conubii* called "a permanent and lasting principle of supernatural life".

The low-key Kantianism which I am talking about, the modern fuzziness that it produces, is more pronounced in the translation of the closing prayer for the Twenty-Fourth Sunday. The authentic text is a euphonious account of grace operative on intelligent being: *"Mentes nostras et corpora possideat, quaesumus, Domine, doni caelestis operatio, ut non noster sensus in nobis, sed eius praeveniat semper effectus."* The request here is that "the operation of the heavenly gift might possess our minds and bodies so that its effects may always prevail over our own understanding". But the translation ignores the point of the prayer against receptionism: "Lord, may the Eucharist you have given us influence our thoughts and actions." There must be a thud in heaven when that prayer arrives.

The Elizabethan translators, even when of misguided views, managed to produce versions more faithful to the theology and cadence of the texts than we enjoy today. Literacy explains only part of the contrast; the modern complex is imbued with an experiential idiom which constrains even the sincerest attempts to represent the sacramental organism of Christ's Body. The result tends to confuse habitual grace with sensible consolations. This has long been the affliction of a certain school of Hinduism which associates the Absolute (Brahman) and the Self (Atman); it has haunted the various forms of enthusiasm in the Christian sects; and unguided by adequate Catholic voices, it has set the tone for the sort of sentimentalism which is still to be found among some intellectuals.

Where metaphysical objectivity does not obtain, any kind of obscurantism can appeal to the intellectual. Surely Cardinal Newman's famous "Definition of a Gentleman" was aimed at this, but his words were so acute that few felt the jab. It is not a prescription for the virtuous ideal; the gentleman of whom he speaks is the nineteenth-century forerunner of the modern nominalist who rejects abstract concepts for particular evidences. At times he is agreeable, but he remains ignorant of the Source of generation. The period known as the Enlightenment provided a philosophical climate for the ephemeral notion of *gens* and gentility. From the human standpoint it could be charming, as when the French translated "Blessed are the meek", Blessed are the debonair. But something dark began to shroud the distinction between an open mind and an empty mind; enlightenment came to have little to do with illumination.

From the background of this sort of milieu, no less distinguished a gentleman than the President of the Johns Hopkins University, Steven Muller, in no less a journal than the *New York Times* (10 November 1985), made a statement which still is tolerable in the academic world: "Only after the Enlightenment was the university set free from the bonds of religious orthodoxy and transformed into an institution of unfettered inquiry." It was tantamount to saying that only after Hansel and Gretel had thrown away their map were they free to get lost in the woods. But the same year, the Pope received that educator and a delegation of scholars from his university in special audience; he addressed them from the chains of belief which bound him, as the teacher of teachers. An editor wrote an article in the university magazine trying to explain the profound impact he had made on that group, moving some to tears. Less than a year later, President Muller spoke in a more sober vein again in the *New York Times* (7 September 1986):

We are very good at training new generations not only to function with what we have discovered but to become discoverers themselves. That's the good news. The bad news is the university has become godless. We must confront so many value issues, from euthanasia to genetic engineering to weapons that can destroy the world, and we no longer have the strong religious rallying point that we had in the nineteenth century. We have to develop a new value system.

Now whether or not a new value system can be developed true to truth about the human condition depends on your concept of orthodoxy. But it does seem that the old concept of orthodoxy is proving to be less harmful to intelligent perception than some recently thought. What exactly is meant by the "unfettered inquiry" to which religious orthodoxy was sacrificed? And why should a Pope so exquisitely bound by religious orthodoxy seem so free? If unfettered inquiry means "learning for learning's sake" it is as constricting as "art for art's sake". When spoken by the artist, that basically means art for the artist's sake; and when the speaker is a curator, it probably means art for the sake of the gallery. Learning for its own sake sounds at first no worse than an innocent hobby. But it as as base and reprehensible as eating for the sake of eating, a cerebral gluttony. In religion, the Church for the Church's sake is clericalism, and it should be slapped down at every opportunity for God's sake. And that is the whole point: the Church is for God's sake as art is for God's sake and learning for God's sake. By this comes the one reason for shouting, "For God's sake, teach!" Otherwise people will worship anything except God who alone is himself for his own sake. The dream of a "free university" is the most polemicized form of education ever devised; and academic freedom as a cause is hardly ever invoked unless it is as a signal for academic privilege. This is so evident that anyone should be a lunatic who denies it; this is not so, however, since clinical lunatics do not have tenure.

Nevertheless, it is lunacy to think that a thing that exists for its own sake is magnanimous, wise, and free.

The Enlightenment restricted perception almost fatally. It was a social version of a solar eclipse, and the eclipse was so total that people in it were considered bright for having the slightest shadow of a doubt. It arrested scientific development at the second level of inquiry, that is, at the level of moral perception; and remained oblivious to the prophetic light. In such shade, the undeveloped man could think himself a perfect gentleman, and the undeveloped woman a perfect lady. It was quite a comedown from the mediaeval romance of the courtly knight and his lady, but it seemed adequate to the occasion. At least those who lived it out had stored enough of the classical patrimony of culture to retain remnants of piety, shreds named order and propriety. Today even the normative ethics are gone. The hedonistic baby-boomers in this last part of the twentieth century believe, with a crude fundamentalism that would have shocked the worst mannerists of the Enlightenment, that "Manners Makyth Man". It is not even a Burkean conservatism, for that could only obtain in Burke's own age when people still knew what to do with their independence. It is really a sad and untutored bestialism that thinks any man or woman is well civilized who is well decorated and well heeled.

Manners that do make the man are the supernatural manners of faith, hope, and love; they are curiosities only to a mind alienated from its own world. St. Peter's word for piety in his Second Letter is *eusebia,* the obligation to participate in universal human experience; anything less is the fantasy of experientialism which, when it tries to be something more, bathes in its own bathos. *Eusebia* is the ascent to the place where the perfect Man bathed in our death. The highest etiquette is sacrifice, and only the most refined citizens of culture know how to get the sacrifice right. Refinement is nothing if it is not *refinar, raffiner, raffinare:* to separate a substance from extraneous matter by the use of heat. We are, so to speak, refined only through fire; and the learned man is one who knows the right way to get burned. The pedant sacrifices others, and flees the purgative good of trial and suffering. This is the paganism of the intellect without God. Unamuno says, "The chiefest sanctity of a temple is that it is a place to which men go to weep in common." The same should be said of the university where the great wail of ignorance is lifted. But if the university abandons God, it has a derelict pietism of its own, and it is the tragic one of men weeping each on his own.

Modernists see what I have described quite differently. Cardinal Journet writes:

> It is not to be believed, say the Modernists, that God has revealed through Christ and the Apostles any definitive truth to be received by the intelligence and preserved intact forever. All that God did—insofar as it is possible to speak of God at all—was to move the souls of the Apostles, and these then attempted to translate their experience into more or less happy conceptual formulas, not in the least to be taken for a "divine law" or as binding on later generations.

Without knowledge of the divine law, the modern thinker is bereft of a workable system of authority; authority is acknowledged as necessary, but it is held suspect, and the use of authority is considered a deficient concession to necessity. A decided neurosis of the secular spirit is its drive to secure the authority for truth in an inadequate source. The American Medical Association recently heard a lecture on medical ethics by an actor who had played a physician on a popular television series. A Congressional agriculture committee received formal testimonies from three Hollywood actresses who had performed the role of farmer's wife in films. The benevolence of their commitments is not important; what does matter is the total fantasy about universal and particular authority.

St. Peter was a teacher by the highest commission, ordered by the Master to instruct the nations. False piety was too trivial for the universal account he had to give; and his own instincts would have to be bound to take him where they would not have him go, but such discipline is the obligation of all erudition, supernatural and natural. The youngest of the apostles knew this as well as his senior: "Every progressive who does not remain in the teaching of Christ does not have God" (2 Jn 9).

Piety is the mortar of culture. By no mean play with words, pietism then is the glue for meagre culturism, by which I mean only habits of culture; they may even be international, but they are not universal because they exist as facts of place, and not of time and truth. The draft document on Catholic schools circulated by the Congregation for Catholic Education in 1985 says this: "Faith . . . to have a decisive force on human realities in order to elevate them, must become culture; a faith which does not become culture is a faith not fully accepted, not wholly thought, not faithfully lived." A faith that does not "become culture" will rapidly be replaced by those culturisms which then function as objects of faith themselves. By this route, some Catholic universities and colleges have compartmentalized the systematic Catholic vision, removing it from the practice of culture. They have become ambiguous institutions with Catholic appurtenances. Catholic parents may continue to send their sons and daughters there by force of habit, just as the generals of the First World War, who knew only mounted combat, kept sending ranks of troops into machine gun flak as though it were still a cavalry charge. They may feel betrayed when the youth return with new and unspeakable wounds, but they will not be certain how to react. Without reform, Catholic colleges are likely to be Catholic only in the remotest sense that Princeton is Presbyterian or Brown is Baptist. But that will have nothing to do with cultural reality.

The change would be more serious in the case of the Catholic university, knowing that Catholicism is the substance of universal associations which originally brought universities into being. That is why, when university scholars instituted the theory of the Death of God, they courted their own demise. Neither God nor the universities died, since the theory was a theology acting according to the rules of natural science, and a natural science with theological pretensions. But systematic thought has to be rehabilitated if the insult which the academy hurled against heaven is not to continue to redound upon itself. Pope John Paul II addressed the Sixth Symposium of the Council of European Episcopal Conferences:

> ... the cultural systems, institutions and ideologies which had characterized the Europe of this century, and originated naive utopias, have gone into crisis under the blows of ... instrumental rationality and of the empire of science and technology. *The university* —that glorious European institution to which the Church gave birth—shows itself incapable of elaborating an acceptable cultural project. This indicates that in modern society culture has failed in its very function as guide.

Already, the cultural initiatives are shifting. Seminal thought and inventive research are taking place less and less in the university; corporations and foundations are shouldering an increasing amount of the responsibility, and certain industrial organizations have begun to grant their own degrees. But the university, as native home of the liberal arts, becomes increasingly calcified as it struggles to maintain its temporalities, even at the expense of quality: one could say, with considerable evidence at hand, that the typical graduate student in any field is less literate than the graduate of a representative high school forty years ago. The American academic establishment is tending toward a tenured social class without much justification. Sixty-five percent of all full-time faculty members in the United States have tenure; over eighty percent at the universities of Wisconsin and Berkeley. There is much to be said for tenure in principle; but on such a scale it could further isolate our colleges. Creative thinkers are forced from the academic nest, leaving behind a flaking carapace called the intellegentsia, much occupied with guarding its privileges, like a hereditary duke struggling to retain the last of his stately homes.

Universal Associations

It is not enough to reform education as a craft. There has to be a reanimation of the duty to transcendence and tribe if the liberal arts are to breathe anew. Anything that becomes its own object distorts itself, the shorthand for which is "ism": without a classical basis for the unity of culture, the best intentions could only fabricate transcendentalism and tribalism.

I recall laboring over Latin gerunds as a twelve-year-old, and diagramming sentences on the blackboard as the teacher tapped her ruler. This was in a public school, the lady was the daughter of a Methodist parson, and a participle seemed to me nothing more than a participle. It was not long ago: the Soviets had just fired off their first Sputnik and the experts were calling for a drastic retooling of the American school system. Miss Evans was impervious to all that. There were those who must have thought her class quaint: the boys and girls, white and black and Jew and Christian, some from old Yankee stock and others newly arrived with names hard to spell; each with chalk writing words that once had reached in frosted breath as far as cold Caledonia, and in sultry speech and languid tones to the high walls of Persepolis. But as I grew up the words kept coming together. By a pattern of events, I found myself living in Rome, and on one occasion part of an amateur marathon. My teacher was as dead as the emperors (I am told that security guards now patrol the corridors of her old school), but I still ran to the rhythm of her iambics. Caesar's rod and Miss Evans' ruler were batons passed on to me. Caesar's gods were not Miss Evans' god; but they both had known in their own days of a greater power that gives the speaker his speech, and of speeches spoken long before and that should be heard again.

The hour the race began at the Colosseum, the crowds were not too different from those who watched Hadrian's twenty-four elephants move the Colossus of Nero, and no less loud than those who cheered his rhinoceros fights. So the runners ran, where horses had run down the Imperial Way, past the Curia where senators had sat with ivory wands awaiting death at the hands of the Gauls; past the prison of St. Peter and the balcony where Paul II applauded his popinjay carnivals. Down the Corso along the Palazzo of the Doria-Pamphilis and the place where St. Paul, they say, wrote of Onesimus to Philemon; past San Marcello where the bizarre Rienzo was hanged, and soon through the "Ecco Roma" gate, the grand entrance to Rome before the combustion engine ruined the world. On to the Milvian bridge where the world was baptized, and along the watery vein of empire, past all the scenes of "Tosca" and up the Campidoglio of Titus, and Charles V and in their steps Mark Clark. Then a final burst onto the Circus Maximus, where instead of laurel the runners got a drink of glucose in orange juice and a certificate from the Bank of Naples.

The appointed reading for Vespers that night was: "Know ye not that they which run in a race run all, but one receives the prize? So run that ye may obtain" (1 Cor 9:24). The prize was not a trinket Caesar pressed upon his friends, or a report card such as one's teacher used to give. I did have a reward from them, though, and it was just this: when I first saw the ancient places, I already knew what they were. My temple was not Caesar's; it was not even the Wesleyan meeting house of Miss Evans; but I believed with both of them that one is obliged to one's god, and that one's blood comes from another's womb, and that one is obliged to all the wombs that ever were. In a language they taught me, and at which I am as poor as I am at running, I could recite on top of the Palatine Hill from the "Carmen Saeculare":

> Alme Sol . . . possis nihil urbe Rome visere maius.
> O beloved Sun . . . may you never be able to see anything greater than Rome.

And you could imagine nearby, Augustus in his homespun tunic playing marbles with the children, weary of the city he had found all brick; and St. Paul writing with a scratchy pen of a city all glorious above. Yet neither would have mocked Horace for singing a song of his town, for each in his own school had learned that an education teaches more than the greatness of things; if it is worthy of the name, it teaches to be great with things.

I expect that the two Smiths, with whom this piece began, have a place with these characters, by virtue of an obligation to experience which is not bias; and by revulsion against the "sophisters and calculators" who lurk in every transition of culture, the pedants and plutocrats whose one influence on learning is to destroy it. If learning is recovered in places of learning, more good people will know what to teach and will teach it well. They will know in what ways Adam Smith and Alfred Smith differed, because they will know the things they held in common, and they will be able to point out their faces in the file of history because they will know that there is a file and that there was a history. And the first principle of good teaching will be a simple one: that the race toward a fleeter and trimmer system of study does not cast away the basic duties which have long directed human attention to the best of what has been said and done.

VI

NEWMAN AND MODERN PERSONALITY

The Mystery of Personality

The many accounts of Cardinal Newman's manner, his look, and above all his voice, might make one think that enough has been said. Those who have studied his most eminent Victorian life (1801–1890) certainly know by now that his voice was as silver and his style crystal. But there are those, among whom is anyone of reason, who would want to know more; and this because, as he stooped somewhat in the pulpit and dimmed the lamp before a sea of undergraduates who were missing their dinner to be there, the silver of the voice mellowed the way gold is meant to; and his clarity was less like a sensible equation and more like a sensible form. This is a mystery of Newman, and the only reason to consider it here is that it is the flashing mystery common to all persons; for want of a name it is unimaginatively called personality. But in modern life it has become the twisted mystery called an enigma and, in some collectivized societies, even an ailment. All the more reason, then, to see what Newman did with it.

But first a qualification. In scholastic terms, personality is not what we normally mean by it at all. Personality, speaking technically, is what underlies what is meant by personality speaking ordinarily. Technical personality differs from existence; existence is a contingent attribute of personality since persons are created. Personality is deeper than existence; it would be more accurate to call it that positive attribute which makes the human an independent subject. Whatever else can be said about it, its very impreciseness is what makes it so definite; it is described by being circumscribed. It can hardly be explained better than to say it is that to which all that pertains to it attaches.

The personality then is not the body or the soul; nor is it consciousness or moral freedom. But we know that it is there, and so we speak of another kind of personality which is an attribute of the deeper metaphysical personality. As a working definition, too slight to fill out a whole system, but what modern use ordinarily means by the term, personality is evidence that we are persons. This is what is indicated when someone speaks of a pleasant personality, or a churlish personality, or having lots of personality. It is not at all what the schoolmen meant by their categories, but St. Thomas Aquinas himself would have known exactly what you meant when you said he had an extraordinary personality. He would have known precisely what you meant by saying anyone *has* a personality; though he was more immediately occupied with how it is that one *is* a personality. Commonly speaking then, which was Newman's method, personality is the vernacular evidence of the speechless soul, the natural expression of the supernatural endowments of will and intellect, much as graciousness is the conspicuous declaration of grace, irrepressible despite its concealments. Man is an unfinished being, but he is not mute. A greatness of Newman for the post-modern observer is the way he represents the personality properly as a spiritual deduction and shows how its development, as any art, attains full worth when it is faithful to a spiritual theme. As every agnostic painting called "Mother and Child" is a surreptitious Madonna and Christ, so the "real character" begrudgingly respected by the cynic is a clandestine ikon.

Any list of Newman's inventive gifts to the contemporary

critic must in some way include the illustration of how the higher reference perdures even as the cultural climate obscures it; into lengthening shadows of modern behaviorism, he pokes the glimmer of a thing good in content and holy in potential. He calls it personality, or human authenticity, and describes it in such a torrent of allusion that one would think the only perfectly mature personality has to be that of the saint. For the saint exhibits perfect individuation free of alienation. And totally out of character, Newman would have pounded loudly on the doors of B. F. Skinner and Carl Rogers alike, to say just that.

To the latest catch-phrase about "growing as a person", Newman would reply that there is no other way to grow; and as for "getting in touch with your feelings", he would say precisely that there is no other way to touch. Actually, the Victorian Liberals anticipated the jumbled thought behind the modern jargon, although they spoke it more elegantly; with modernists they shared the mistaken idea of perfection as endless growth rather than the attainment of an end so that the substance of perfection is "not a having and a lasting but a growing and a becoming". That expression is not from the latest suburban sensitivity session; it belongs to Matthew Arnold. Supposedly, everyone knows that *persona* is defective until it obliges *personaliter*. But this is common sense only because there is an uncommon reason behind it. If the modern optimist saw the personality as a puzzle, the Christian knows it to be a mystery. For a mystery does not affront reason; but it compels the reason to acknowledge a depth beyond observable reference. Newman compares mystery to an island which seems to be alone and wafted in the water but which is the summit of a submerged mountain range. A mystery, we should then say, is the sort of mountain you do not climb, but descend, to conquer. This is the principle of depth psychology, the important though incomplete modern pursuit of the essential person. And it is more profoundly acted out in the divine pursuit of man in the Incarnation. The self knows only part of itself until it acknowledges its unseen self. The cry of the isolated is "I want to be me." Newman would persist: "Who else can you be?" But only the true principles beneath becoming and being, underlying contingency and its source, can make the man on an island a man on a mountain, like St. Paul: "It is no longer I who live but Christ who lives in me" (Gal 2:20). This is the descent from the topical ego to the fundament of being. Newman's own life models what that means for human rehabilitation at the end of modernity.

Personality and the Operation of Grace

The world works as a sacramental economy; and human participation in it hinges on the distinction between subjectivism and personalism. An *ennui* of alienation sets the pervasive mood of moderns because the hinge has been broken. Newman dedicated himself to an exposition of certitude as a thing other than the "notional" impressionism of the nineteenth-century Liberal school which sowed the seeds of modernism as the theological part of cultural modernity. And he proceeded to a fact which is almost too subtle for the secularized intellect and it is this: the phenomenon of revelation is a "method of personation" culminating in the evidence of the divine Word as an uttering person. Consequently, all truly perceptive life is the "service of a person".[1] No social system and no expression of an idea is valid if it does not authenticate personal dignity.

The deliberate will of God had made "Men, not angels, the

[1] *U.S.,* pp. 28–29.

Ministers of the Gospel".[2] Personality, again in the vernacular since technically personality is the subject of character as an attribute, is a display of the unique character of a life for which Christ died, and thus can help mediate virtue; it is also a fallible vehicle of perception in consequence of original sin, and so it can impede the operation of any virtue. Though grace as the motive of virtue is a divine donation, it is received efficaciously in the measure by which faith obliges the personality to the will of Christ in the sacraments.

Now this touches a touchy subject. The Sacramentalist with his concern for the agency *operato,* and the Pietist with his regard for the agency *operantis,* both at various times in their formulations, have been tempted to overlook the complementary principle which holds that the faith of the individual cannot be divorced from the faith of the Church. The "secret power of divine grace" is discerned in realizing that God looks in gratuitous love upon "the hidden man of the heart", and of this love "the visible Church is the expression, the protection, the instrumental cause, and the outward perfection".[3]

In his *Lectures on Justification,* Newman denies Luther any right to his narrow sense of private faith in commentary, for example, on the Pauline epistles; but Newman also rejects any ecclesial tendency to eradicate the commitments of singular personality. The effective operation of grace in the Church rather requires of the personality its perfection by faith through voluntary submission to the likeness of Christ. While there are saints who, through the pursuit of a mystical course, seem to need no earthly sustenance and have no apparent natural affection (for example, St. John, St. Mary Magdalen, the hermits, and many of the holy virgins), there is a second class of saints

[2] *Mix.,* p. 45.
[3] *S.V.O.,* p. 58.

in dignity equal to the first who "do not put away their natural endowments, but use them to the glory of the Giver" and who are "only made more eloquent, more poetical, more profound, more intellectual, by reason of their being more holy". Among these Newman ranks St. John Chrysostom (who "by his sweetness and naturalness compels one's devotion"), St. Athanasius, and "above all" St. Paul the Apostle.[4] Detachment from the tainted things of the world is not detachment from colorful characteristics of the self. As you read the *Historical Sketches,* you can picture Newman's silhouette against the profile of St. Gregory who looms "as great theologically as he is personally winning".[5] And as much as we stand in awe of the Jesuits among us, it is a matter of record that Newman admired Loyola but chose to walk with the sons of Neri who seemed possibly kinder, slightly more cheerful, and much better musicians. He prayed to St. Philip that we might "Not be the cold sons of so fervent a Father".[6]

He is capable of saying to a congregation:

... the prophets have ordinarily not only gifts but graces; they are not only inspired to know and to teach God's will, but inwardly converted to obey it. For surely those can only preach the truth who duly feel it personally; those only transmit it fully from God to men, who have in the transmission made it their own.[7]

In words significant for any Hegelian enthusiast or some liberation theologians, he warns: "No great work was done by

[4] Ibid., pp. 92–93; JHN to J. L. Patterson, January 30, 1867, in Wilfrid Ward, *The Life of John Henry Cardinal Newman,* II (New York: 1912), p. 134.

[5] *H.S.,* II, p. 93.

[6] *Meditations and Devotions of the Late Cardinal Newman* (London: 1911), p. 259.

[7] *Mix.,* p. 364.

a system; whereas systems rise out of individual exertions", a sentiment similar to his famous line: "... no martyr will die for a conclusion". The truth is communicated in human discourse through the "antagonistic principle of personality".[8] This is no dialectic other than the dialect of conscience: *cor ad cor loquitur.*[9] His natural affinity for the Alexandrian school and for the vibrancy of the primitive Church, he acknowledges, was influenced by a "preference of the Personal to the Abstract"; and his accord with Keble, recounted in the *Apologia,* stood on a fundamental epistemology:

> It is faith and love which give to probability a force which it has not in itself. Faith and love are directed towards an Object; in the vision of the Object they live; it is that Object, received in faith and love, which renders it reasonable to take probability as sufficient for internal conviction. Thus the argument from Probability, in the matter of religion, became an argument from Personality, which in fact is one form of the argument from Authority.[10]

In this certainly lies a clue to what so many have called, hardly without exaggeration, the "enchantment" of his oratorical diction. It is not true, as some of the same have claimed in fits of piety, that his public recitations involved "the complete elimination of the personality of the reader". It is true that Newman would have been petrified by the current vulgar idea that lectors in the Liturgy have to "put feeling" into what they are reading. The defective personalism of some modern liturgists would be a torment to his refinements. Yet through, and not in spite of, his naked diffidence, one was aware of God the

---

[8] *Apo.,* pp. 27–28; *G.A.,* p. 93.

[9] See Philip Boyce, "John Henry Newman a Cardinal: One Hundred Years Ago", in the *Clergy Review,* LXIV, 12 (December 1979), p. 431.

[10] *Apo.,* pp. 18–19.

Creator speaking "as He speaks through creation ... by the articulate voice of man". The more he effaced himself, the more one "thought only of the majestic soul that saw God". Here was the antagonistic principle of personality at work, quite as it had been the guiding method of the *Tracts:* it was no "private motive, and no personal aim" but an attempt through the imagination to render an abstraction persuasive, to create "a living Church, made of flesh and blood, with voice, complexion, and motive and action, and a will of its own".[11]

He proclaimed with wry astonishment "to the last" a total obliviousness to the power his personality had over others of whom "of late years I have read and heard that they even imitated me in various ways." Friends held this from him because they "knew too well how disgusted I should be at such proceedings". He took it as a case of how an intrusive personality, not submissive to a higher will, diverts men from God. Personality disintegrates when the empirical ego becomes an imperial ego. In the proper scheme, though he would have denied the choice of example, the effect *ex opere operantis* should be as an elderly woman described it to Cosmo Gordon Lang: "Mr. Newman used to wear a rather dirty surplice, but when he read the lessons we thought he was in heaven."[12]

[11] Ibid., p. 48. Cf. Fathers of the Oratory: *Sermon Notes of Cardinal Newman* (New York: 1913), p. xii; William Lockhart, in *Correspondence of John Henry Newman with John Keble and Others,* 1839–1845, (London: 1917), pp. 390–91.

[12] The report of one of his parishioners, given to the Archbishop and in turn to R. D. Middleton, *Newman and Bloxam: An Oxford Friendship* (London: 1947), pp. 12–13.

Personal and Sacramental Character

Few, if any, of his fellow Catholics preached as regularly as he
on the biblical and patristic understanding of what we now
call the integral personality. The personal element, which he
condemned in its severely individualistic form among the
Protestants, found its proper display in the eschatological dimension of sacramental life. But his experience had taught him to
reverence the place of faith in this economy and not to set up
personal character as an absolute contradiction of sacramental
character. While he condemned in Protestantism "the flocking
to preachers rather than to sacraments (as if the servant were
above the Master, who is Lord over His own house)", he also
admitted that "it is not an easy matter to determine that the
self-appointed preachers in question do really convert the hearts
of men, that is, *do* cast out devils, do work miracles, as they say
they do".[13]

Lacking is the objective certitude of the operation, for as he
summons Prayer Book Englishness to say, "what seems good, is
often not good." The certitude is to be had through the
universal testimony of the Church, without which the individual who is made in the image of God easily degenerates into a
reflection of private error. But the individualistic confidence in
justification gained by faith as by an instrument, *ex opere
operantis,* is not in itself without Catholic substance. For example,
the "benefit arising from the use of holy water accrues not *ex
opere operato,* nor by means of the element itself, but *ex opere
operantis,* through the devout mental acts of the person using it,
and the prayer of the Church".[14] Such is the normal case with

[13] *V.M.* II, p. 39; *P.S.* pp. 192–3. Cf. Placid Murray, *Newman the
Oratorian* (Dublin: 1969), p. 47.
[14] *Diff.* I, p. 85.

sacramentals (although he does not use that term here), but it also pertains to the sacraments themselves. Baptism by water regenerates *ex opere operato;* but, under prescribed conditions, the same effect may be had through baptism by blood. And " . . . the Sacrifice of the Mass benefits the person for whom it is offered *ex opere operato,* whatever be the personal character of the celebrant",[15] but it benefits him more or less, *ex opere operantis,* according to the degree of sanctity which he has attained, and the earnestness by which he offers it.

By an epistemology which locates the image of God in the conscience rather than in the pure mind, it was inevitable that Newman would bring to his description of the Catholic economy an especially high estimation of the personal character as an influence in perception. Theological modernists, through a lack of his subtlety, came to think that this confirmed their liberalism when it was in fact its precise refutation. Through the intuition of God as an acting, judging person instead of a static essence, it follows that we come to encounter him in acts and choices. The idea compares with St. Thomas' concept of God as existence but also differs in the account of apprehension. In the Scholastic tradition, individual acts cannot be diverse or false since we judge by acquired species instead of a subjective intuition; for Newman there is a closer identity between the individual who acts and the image for which he acts. The individual alone is able to know his perception of God. On the other hand, the universal validity of the perception can be determined objectively only by its harmony with the faith of the Church. In this association of the individual *ex operantis*

---

[15] Ibid., p. 86. This helped him as a Catholic to explain how he had been devoted to the Anglican Eucharist; grace had been at work but, separated from the indefectable prayer of the Church, it had come in the Anglican ordinance *ex opere operantis* and not *operato:* v. *Diff.* I, pp. 81–82; Murray, op. cit., pp. 69, 124.

ecclesiae, Newman delivered himself from the subjectivism of which he was often accused but which he professed himself to abhor.[16]

In the particular case of the preacher, but with application to all who confess the Faith, Newman says "he comes to his hearers . . . with antecedents".[17] The choice of words is significant. The sacerdotal kingship of Christ is in the line of Melchizedek who has no personal associations or antecedents; but it is no less for that attached to a prophetic tradition in which personal commitments are instruments of inspired communication:

> . . . people are drawn and moved, not simply by what is said,
> but by how it is said and who says it. The same things said by
> one man are not the same as when said by another.[18]

The inspired word is "but a dead letter (ordinarily considered), except as transmitted from one mind to another".[19] The transmission is the means of "real assent" as opposed to "notional assent" and affects the speaker as well as the hearer, for the preacher may grow in faith even as he preaches: "What is so powerful an incentive to preaching as the sure belief that it is the preaching of the truth?"[20] In this is the key to the impression Newman gave of being part of his own audience, and established a method of which the modern media evangelists often are sad caricatures. Froude said: "He seemed to be addressing the most secret consciousness of each of us, as the

[16] Cf. Harold Weatherby, *Cardinal Newman and His Age* (Nashville: 1973), pp. 200–1.

[17] *Idea,* p. 425.

[18] Ibid.

[19] *U.S.,* p. 95.

[20] *Mix.,* p. 18.

eyes of a portrait appear to look at every person in a room."[21] Father Neville remembered Newman instructing him: "Let me know where [the undergraduates] sit in the Church, that I may picture beforehand how I shall have to stand when I preach, in order to see them naturally, and address them."[22]

What is this but the practical working out of the movement from notion to reality? Notional assent, which consists in self-contemplation, becomes "real" when the mind attends to external objects represented by an impression left as part of one's entire existence, and so it affects the total personality and is not exclusively a matter of the intellect.[23] If his analysis of the "antecedent" process lost anything by being pre-Freudian as a moral psychology, it gained more by being pre-Determinist. The rhetorical Newman was his theory of cognition on display.

Working from the premise of grace operative through discourse, he developed his "most characteristic and effective" technique, namely the exposition of his listener's own reactions to doctrine; he "crystallizes the question, or problem, or truth in such a personal way that the answer itself has an immediate and personal significance".[24] Had modernist theologians chastened their bureaucratic reformism with this method, they might have accomplished better reforms. But the gift for

[21] J. A. Froude, *Short Studies on Great Subjects,* IV (London. 1883), p. 278.

[22] Conversation on April 6, 1867, in *Ward* II, op. cit., p. 138. Cf. M. Nedoncelle, Introduction to *Sermons Universitaires* (Bruges: 1955), p. 7.

[23] See Peter Collins, "Newman and Contemporary Education" in *Educational Theory,* XXVI (February 1976), p. 366; *G.A.,* pp. 79ff.

[24] Eugene M. Burke, "The Salvation of the Hearer" in *American Essays for the Newman Centennial,* ed. J. K. Ryan and E. D. Benard (Washington, D.C.: 1942), pp. 92–93. See, e.g., *S.V.O.,* pp. 1ff.: "Intellect, the Instrument of Religious Training".

empathy was precisely a gift and not a device. Newman described it in one of his own sermons:

> ... do you not know what it is to so love and live upon a person who is present to you, that your eyes follow his, that you read his soul, that you see its changes in his countenance, that you anticipate his wants, that you are sad at his sadness, troubled when he is vexed, restless when you cannot understand him, relieved, comforted when you have cleared up the mystery?[25]

He actually entitled one sermon "Personal Influence, the Means of Propagating the Truth"[26] in oblique tribute to the Aristotelian philosophy of rhetoric to which he never lacked recourse:

> The ethos of the speaker is a cause of persuasion when the speech is so uttered as to make him worthy of belief; for as a rule we trust men of probity more, and more quickly, about things in general, while on points outside the realm of exact knowledge, where opinion is divided, we trust them absolutely.[27]

"Thus", writes Sillem, "he preferred St. John Chrysostom, whom he felt he knew, to Aquinas, whom he never did come to know personally.... He sought objective truth by the method of dialogue, in and through the experience of inter-subjectivity (to use the modern jargon), that is to say in the intercourse of man with man, and the action of mind with mind."[28]

This has its limits. As early as the *Parochial Sermons,* he observed:

[25] *S.V.O.,* p. 36.

[26] *U.S.,* pp. 91ff.

[27] Aristotle, *Rhetoric,* tr. Lane Cooper (New York: 1932), pp. 8–9. On *ethos,* cf. Werner Jaeger, *Paideia, the Ideals of Greek Culture,* I (Oxford: 1945), p. 20.

[28] Edwin Sillem, ed., *The Philosophical Notebook of John Henry Newman* (Louvain: 1969), p. 8. Cf. "St. Paul's Gift of Sympathy" in *S.V.O.,* pp. 106ff.

The religious history of each individual is as solitary and complete as the history of the world. Each man will, of course, gain more knowledge as he studies Scripture more, and prays and meditates more; but he cannot make another man wise or holy by his own advance in wisdom or holiness.[29]

But if one cannot compel, one may encourage. If the rod is not at hand, there is always the staff. So Newman made St. Philip Neri the telling model for his technique with souls, in a description useful for the pastor of post-modern souls:

[Neri] preferred to yield to the stream, and direct the current, which he could not stop, of science, literature, art and fashion, and to sweeten and to sanctify what God had made very good and man had spoilt . . . he would be but an ordinary individual priest as others: and his weapons should be but unaffected humility and unpretending love. All he did was to be done by the light, fervour, and convincing eloquence of his personal character and his easy conversation.[30]

The subjective influence of the subjective character, then, had a certain objectivity, even when it could not claim to effect actual sanctifying grace in the manner of the sacraments themselves. Empathy promotes a widespread sympathy for acts of virtue, disposing a soul toward grace. Newman composed this prayer for his own use, and in our day that celebrated embodiment of empathy, Mother Teresa of Calcutta, has mandated its use by the Missionaries of Charity as a thanksgiving after Mass:

Make me preach Thee without preaching—not by words, but by my example, and by the catching force, the sympathetic

[29] P.S. VII, p. 248. In the sermon "The Individuality of the Soul" he says: "We cannot understand that a multitude is a collection of immortal souls."

[30] Idea, pp. 235–36.

influence, of what I do—by my visible resemblance to Thy saints, and the evident fulness of the love which my heart bears to Thee.[31]

As a visual aid, there could be nothing so direct as the word-picture he creates to describe the priest in the Liturgy, and these comments remain tenable despite the onslaught of some contemporary liturgical abuses:

> Clad in his sacerdotal vestments, [the priest] sinks what is individual in himself altogether, and is but the representation of Him from whom he derives his commission. His words, his tones, his actions, his presence, lose their personality; one bishop, one priest, is like another; they all chant the same notes, and observe the same genuflexions, as they give one peace and one blessing, as they offer one and the same sacrifice. The Mass must not be said without a Missal under the priest's eye; nor in any language but that in which it has come down to us from the early hierarchies of the Western Church. But, when it is over, and the celebrant has resigned the vestments proper to it, then he resumes himself, and comes to us in the gifts and associations which attach to his person. He knows his sheep, and they know him; and it is this direct bearing of the teacher on the taught, of his mind upon their minds, and the mutual sympathy which exists between them which is his strength and influence when he addresses them. They hang upon his lips as they cannot hang upon the pages of his book.[32]

Current trivializations of worship have reversed this order, unduly personalizing the canonical parts even while bureaucratizing the pastoral facts. But if Newman's description survived the romantic excesses of his own day, it is likely to surmount the balloon Masses and bubbly Catechisms of ours.

[31] *Meditations and Devotions,* op. cit., p. 365.
[32] *Idea.,* pp. 425–26.

The Consecration of Personality

The *Apologia* was Newman's fitting equivalent of a *Summa* since only the personal exposition of his own character's formation could be an adequate vehicle for that idealist epistemology modified by a sensationalist psychology with which he described individual assent to divine propositions. It was a complete rejection of abstract and rationalist philosophies in favor of a personalist theory by which the individual grasps the truth by reasoning in response to definite points. Psychological and phenomenological as the approach was, it was also metaphysical since the entire order had been constructed through the providence of God. Integral conduct cannot be anthropocentric.[33]

As a pioneer in theological anthropology, Newman was a precursor of the personalist method of Pope John Paul II. The Cardinal's appeal to patrology as a way of personalizing Thomist realism parallels the Pope's post-modern reference to the phenomenological existentialists for the same purpose. The great issues of human consciousness, participation in history, man and the moral good, figure large for both. The author of the *Grammar of Assent* might have called *The Acting Person* in some way his own. Wojtyla's collaborator, Mieczyslaw Krapiec of the University of Lublin, may be doing by the philosophical anthropology of his book *I–Man* what Newman undertook in the *Development of Doctrine*. Not for nothing has Wojtyla matched Newman's enthusiasm for inventive literary drama, the most instinctive vehicle for expounding the phenomenon of consciousness.

[33] Cf. Charles Dessain, "Cardinal Newman Considered as a Prophet" in *Concilium*, 7, 4 (September 1968), p. 42. Cf. Vatican Secretariat for Non-Christians, "Toward the Meeting of Religions" (September 21, 1967).

Newman's affinity for the Oratorian ideal, albeit clerical, and his principles in *Consulting the Laity,* gave off sparks of that existentialist personalism which has motivated Pope John Paul's promotion of lay spirituality through movements which confound many clericalists who at the moment are still trying to address a modernity which they do not realize is coming apart. Newman might have said in similar language what Wojtyla said some time before ascending the Petrine throne:

> We maintain the principle of personalism against that of individualism and totalitarianism. Both these conceptions destroy in the human person the possibility and even the ability of participation. They deprive man of his rights to participation.[34]

The Pope's "Lublin Thomism" is to some degree the fruition of what we might call Newman's "Birmingham Thomism".

Although Newman intimated the election in this century of a pope from a distant land, he did not defer his personalism theme to a later and greater authority. It reverberated in his first book when he said that revelation serves men in the way it "clears up all doubts about the existence of God as separate from and independent of nature; and shows that the world depends, not merely on a system, but on a Being, real, living and individual".[35] The reason no one will be a martyr for a conclusion is that martyrs in one sense are the conclusion. The conclusion is the resolution of an affinity for something greater than the self. Christian martyrs conclude the indwelling in their souls of the Holy Spirit himself and, through him, of the indwelling of the Father and the Son. The life of grace, which frees the person from the tyranny of the "I", also introduces the personality to the friendship of the "Thou".

---

[34] See David Q. Liptak, "The Pope's Personalism" in *The* [Hartford] *Catholic Transcript,* 8 February 1980.

[35] *Arians,* p. 184.

Newman rejected any Nonconformist tendency to stress belief rather than the object of belief (which is why he objected to Evangelicals who preached "conversion" instead of Christ), and he opposed any proclivity among Catholics to portray grace as some kind of autonomous quality or entity in the soul. Justification could mean but one thing, and all accounts of grace had to heed it: " . . . to receive the divine presence within us, and to be made a temple of the Holy Ghost". Grace is "a personal favour, a loving presence" and thus Newman, in the words of Dessain, "refused to separate the presence of God as a friend from the change in his creation that was a consequence of that presence".[36] In complement to this reality, he embarked upon a career of mortification which has been much ignored by biographers; this meant, of course, the constant mortifications of temperament in his dealings with others, but also corporal mortifications including the fervent use of the discipline. As early as *Tract* 21, it was recognized that no saint had made the mistake of denying death to the lower senses.[37] Decline of the interior life of the soul, and especially in the religious orders in modern experience, is directly attributable to that inflated error. Religious communities which were meant to contradict the age have become refuges for the utopian egoism of the modern age. The egoism permeates society, so that from the unmotivated cleric to the hyperactive "young urban professional", the personality provides the world little because the person is almost primarily occupied with consuming. Every instance of decadence in piety is evidence of an attempt to replace habitual grace with constant gratification. A neurotic personality consumes distractions because it is bored; the weaker

---

[36] Dessain, op. cit., p. 42.

[37] On mortification, cf. *Tracts* 14, 18, 21, 66, 86; *Letters and Diaries,* V, pp. 1–2; also Meriol Trevor, *The Pillar of the Cloud,* pp. 203–4, 332, 453–4, 538–9.

the personality the more likely is it to seek consolation in trends. The consecrated life is nothing if it does not contradict this banality. Newman knew this in his own age but would surely have been astonished at how Catholics themselves have become symptomatic of ephemeralness in the present age. The Preacher called this "vanity of vanities". That means: a man who will not conclude who he is, will always behave as a hypothesis.

Positively speaking, Newman's model of total psychological consecration has had an enormous effect on Christian apologetics, not only schematically as with the highest voices in the Church, but also methodically in the case of modern writers who have been compelled both by Newman's grasp of being and the way he expressed it: Gerard Manley Hopkins, Hilaire Belloc, G. K. Chesterton, Evelyn Waugh, the early Graham Greene, Paul Claudel, Flannery O'Connor, and, perhaps even through more obscure associations, Sigrid Undset. Words of Newman have their place in the modern literary canon, so that:

> ... the more a man is educated, whether in theology or secular science, the holier he needs to be if he would be saved. That devotion and self rule are worth all the intellectual cultivation in the world. That in the case of most men literature and science and the habits they create, so far from ensuring these highest of gifts, indispose the mind towards their acquisition.[38]

God has made man to become man, not half a man or a man arrested in conscience, but a man alive to authenticity. Within this comprehensive outlook, Newman's Christian humanism influenced some practical advice on the training of youth. The Oratory School at Birmingham had a remarkably free system of regulations, for instance. It represents his respect for the

[38] J. H. Newman to W. Ward in *Ward* I, op. cit., pp. 515–16.

natural endowments of the soul, a theme to be amplified by the teaching of Vatican II and the Revised Code of Canon Law on personal freedom. The natural man has an autonomy of his own: " . . . he is this sentient, intelligent, creative and operative being, quite independent of any extraordinary help from Heaven or any definite religious belief. . . . "[39] This is not anthropocentricism; it is sheer sensible anthropology. On the specific matter of priestly formation, he writes this most delightful passage in a private letter:

> I have little belief in true vocations being destroyed by contact with the world—I don't mean contact with sin and evil—but contact with the world which consists of such intercourse as is natural and necessary. . . . The thought is awful, that boys should have had no trial of their heart, till at the end of some years, they go out into the world with the most solemn vows upon them, and then perhaps for the first time learn that the world is not a seminary. . . . Moreover I dread too early a separation from the world for another reason—for the spirit of formalism, affectation, and preciseness, which it is so very apt to occasion.[40]

He was equally convinced, more than most intellectuals in his era, of progressivist optimism, that man has to be taught himself anew, recovering what he has lost of self-knowledge through the "form of infidelity of the day" which we would call secular humanism. As sin imposes an unrelieved conformity upon souls, so true maturation in holiness secures the most creative individuality, which is greatly different from individualism: "Moses does not write as David; nor Isaiah as Jeremiah; nor St. John as St. Paul. . . . Each has his own manner, each speaks his own words, though he speaks the while the words

[39] *Idea.*, p. 222. Cf. ibid., p. 234: "She [the Church] fears no knowledge, but she purifies all; she represses no element of our nature, but cultivates the whole."

[40] J. H. Newman to Bellasis in *Ward* I, op. cit., p. 595.

of God. They speak for themselves . . . with their own arguments, with their own deductions, with their own mode of expression."[41] Newman simply witnesses to the elementary principle of redemption: *gratia non tollit naturam sed perficit.* Grace, both sanctifying and habitual, delivers the personality from the worst of all tyrannies, slavery to the self. Slavery such as this masquerades as a species of liberation when, in fact, it is an arrested development. The less mature the personality is, the more anonymous it seems. There are no two saints alike; this cannot be said of sinners. Unaided by grace, the fact of individuation as the principle of personality yields to the impersonal conceit of the mob.

In the *Apologia,* for instance, the noble characters are singular, like the most accomplished Augustan portrait busts; and the baleful ones woven in and out of Newman's gossamer pages are more like stereotypes of certain pathologies and less like heroically tragic figures. Were the writing superficial, the sadder characters would be brighter and more interesting; but it is precisely because Newman is so careful to reveal all that can be revealed that he exposes the illusion of the vibrant muddle and original cliché. What is his right to do this, but that egoism is not self-absorption, for it is really absorption in everything else as though it were the self? So the victim gains the whole world and loses his own soul in the transaction. The egoist in fact betrays the vital ego by behaving as though the self were anything but the self. Newman marked it among those of his own day who defined themselves as Gentlemen, and he would observe it today in the Determinist who cannot organize his own life and so decides to restructure Guatemala. Once a party or a nation or an economic theory substitutes for the person, then it is easy to conclude that God himself is a human self-

[41] *Mix.,* pp. 367–8.

projection. That merely shows too high an opinion of the self, or too low an opinion of the projection. In any case, it disorders the person and disorients the personality. On a cosmic scale, this makes Hell the state where persons are alone together. Whatever its music, it must be in the portable headsets you see on people today walking through street crowds as though there were no crowds. Here is the high-tech repetition of the Heraclitean inability to answer the question of the one and the many.

Newman had seen his culture already in need of this remonstrance as it was fast abandoning, through the negligence of Liberal individualists who thought that contingent being can be its own source of perfection, both the cosmic sense of creation in the sacramental order and kinetic personalism as it obtained in the classical assumptions about universal man. The first stabs of modernity were aggravating an old moral wound:

> ... Cicero says that Plato and Demosthenes, Aristotle and Isocrates might have respectively excelled in each other's province, but that each was absorbed in his own; his words are emphatic; "quorum uterque, suo studio delactatus, *contemsit* alterum". Specimens of this peculiarity occur every day. You can hardly persuade some men to talk about any thing but their own pursuit; they refer the whole world to their center, and measure all matters by their own rule, like the fisherman in the drama, whose eulogy of his deceased lord was, that "he was so fond of fish".[42]

Something like the fisherman was the radical feminist who recently wrote of an indulgent bishop: "He affirmed me in my okay-ness."

The Ciceronian spectrum, as it shone on mediaeval and renaissance horizons, was vanishing around Newman, and he

---

[42] *Idea.*, pp. 399–400.

could detect the rudiments of a new thing cruel in its vapidity:
a society little offended by heresy and schism because it has
little commitment to truth and unity, disposed to collectivism
because it cannot comprehend universality. This was his intimation of what would come to be called the post-Christian age
by moderns whose confidence at this very moment is being
shattered by somewhat more reflective thinkers who are coming to call themselves post-modern.

As we have approached his theory of personality, we have
done that theory little credit unless we see that we have been
discussing Newman himself. And if his theory is that personality can be a power, then he is that theory's proof. The way the
very recollection of his name compels us to think about this, is
proof of the proof. The more he sought to disappear, the more
vividly he emerged as testament to the force of "unaffected
humility and unpretending love".

In the youth of his maturity, he had gazed at his audience
with bright eyes in a dim light; in the fullness of that maturity,
he watched another audience more dimly in a brighter light.
When the eyes at last were shut, Cardinal Manning, who did
not often give the impression of eagerness to place the light of
Newman on a lampstand, swept aside the external dispositions
which impede the sympathy of great men for each other: "A
noble and beautiful life is the most convincing and persuasive
of all preaching, and we have all felt its power."

This was a fair thing to say of one whose personality may
yet be judged by the Church to bear the stamp of heroic
purity, humility, and devotion. If so, the great Church post-
modern will know universally what the little pre-modern
congregation of Littlemore knew precisely when it was parted
long ago from one who "told you what you knew about
yourself or what you did not know; has read to you your
wants or feelings, and comforted you by the very reading. . . . "

VII

THE SHALLOW RADICALS

Radical Theology

When some sermons tend to be essays, an essay might be indulged for being something of a sermon. At least this one begins with a text:

> There shall come forth a shoot from the stump of Jesse,
>   and a branch shall grow out of his roots.
> And the Spirit of the Lord shall rest upon him,
>   the spirit of wisdom and understanding,
>   the spirit of counsel and might,
>   the spirit of knowledge, piety, and the fear of the Lord.
>
> (Is 11:1–3)

Theological inquiry looks to the roots of the branch; it is concerned with the initial source of consequent beings. The roots of reality are its proper subject, and as such it is the definitive radicalism. But it loses its radical quality if it is diverted from those roots. There are, then, no "theologies"; no theology of education, no theology of nature, no theology of peace and justice. There are pedagogies, ecologies, sociologies, and forensics. Without theological reference, they are branches without roots; but they are not theologies. They have to do with attributes and circumstances of God's creation; they are not initially about God. Nor is there black theology or white theology, but only theology done by blacks and whites; just as technically speaking, there are no "Gospels" but only *the* Gospel according to Matthew or

Mark or Luke or John. But no one has a theology of his own, as no one has a gospel of his own. Theology is *logos theou,* the study of God.

The word spoken about God is accurate to the extent that it comes from God. He is the Word, and so he qualifies words about himself. Such science is of an order different from any other; even when it is "natural", it is only so as an approach to revealed utterances. The radical revelation is aided in its perception by the spiritual gifts proclaimed by Isaiah the Prophet, encompassing the whole endowment of Jewish history. The gifts to Solomon: wisdom and understanding. The gifts to David: counsel and might. The gifts to the Prophets: knowledge, piety, and fear of the Lord. Altogether, they create that "poverty of spirit" which, in the happy translation of the New English Bible, is the knowledge of one's need of God (Mt 5:3; cf. Lk 6:20).

Without that spiritual poverty, the mind does not know the joy of needing roots. It simply diverts itself with various novelties. The "rich who have their reward" and the "rich who are sent empty away" are those whose heads are in the clouds where their hearts should be. The modern quest for "meaningful" items and attractions is nothing other than a lack of spiritual poverty. And since spiritual poverty is the highest wealth, to be its opposite is not to be rich but to be ephemeral.

Now, the pursuit of novelty is not quite the same as attraction to the exotic, which can intimate some impulse of grace, testimony that "here we have no continuing city" (Heb 13:14). But the rapture of novelty is infantile, and the faddist is an adult victim of immaturity. When faddism becomes a habit, it becomes a terminal illness of the spirit, and holds virtue suspect. Its heroes usually are sardonic; it thinks boredom is more sophisticated than laughter; the tavern humor of W. C. Fields appeals to it more than the tavern humor of G. K. Chesterton.

It seems to be interested principally in not being interested: diversion is the one thing that rivets its attention. The electronic media exercise a considerable influence over people for this reason: once someone cares more about what is new than what is good, any news is thought to be good for being new. And in a perverse way, the worse the news, the better. It is true that no one puts new wine into old wineskins; but modernity has made a technology of putting new wine into nothing at all, and then wonders why the technologists' feet get wet.

News reporters have assumed a prominent role in theology; it is possible for a newspaper of record, for instance, to create a theological movement. It may be, to take a case, that Jürgen Moltmann would have remained outside the American intellectual consciousness in the late 1960s had not a New York newspaper run a column about him on its front page. William Randolph Hearst is said to have given orders to "puff" the relatively unknown Billy Graham on a slow news day in the late 1940s. Dr. Moltmann and Dr. Graham, for all their disparity, are eminent gentlemen and the press was not guilty of a social crime in their publicity. The popularization of the "Death of God" writers was of a different order; yet the wild attention given them seems quaint at the remove of only these few years. Names like William Hamilton, Thomas Alitzer, and John Robinson are curiosities today, but curious for not having turned out to be the radicals which celebrity called them.

The "Death of God" adventure was a case of the Paralysis of Man. But whatever else it was, it was not theology, nor were its teachers theologians. I do not mean this in a derogatory way; only in what should be an incontestable sense, like saying Christian Scientists are not pathologists. Theology is the science of God, and not the science of the absence of God. And a theologian is not one who is qualified to do theology; a theologian is one who does theology. That is not an argument for a closed shop; it is a form of argument against a closed mind. And as theology is the science of God, it cannot be the science of Professor Quodlibet's opinion of God; although proper theology should give at least an expectation of God's opinion of Professor Quodlibet.

There is, then, no Radical Theology opposed to other theology. Radical Theology is like Wet Water. If theology does not racinate, it is dilettantish; and our Creator is not a dilettante, even though the heavens sing out that he made us in his image. If humans are poor images, what of that? The one thing it would mean is that there are no vague theologies, only vague theologians. God is not what his creatures make him out to be, but what he is: "I am what I am" (Ex 3:14). And an apocryphal spirit could add: "Even if you don't like it."

The Real Way the World Works

Theologians of Jewish-Christian perception respond to fact because their theology is complected by history. This is somewhat difficult to appreciate in a syncretistic and relativistic environment. In the heady sequence of nominalism, modern becomes modernism; science, scientism; piety, pietism. History then runs the risk of historicism, which treats truths as fragile compositions of their particular ages. But the theologian is responsible to the integrity of history as the vehicle of God's immutable revelation; and the Lord of history employs the facts of history to disabuse anyone of denying that. When Peter, with James and John, proposed to erect three "booths" after the Transfiguration—something like the chapels at the Kennedy International Airport—Christ rained audacious wisdom on them from above: "And when they lifted up their eyes, they saw no one but Jesus only" (Mt 17:8; Mk 9:8;

Lk 9:36). When Peter pontificated, saying that Jerusalem was not part of the eschatological order, Christ rang out: "You are a hindrance to me; for you are not on the side of God, but of men" (Mt 16:23). On the road to Emmaus, the very Word interrupted the convoluted catechesis of the two disciples: "O foolish men, and slow of heart to believe all that the prophets have spoken!" (Lk 24:25). And what surely must have been the most celestial theological seminar: "Afterward he appeared to the eleven themselves as they sat at table; and he upbraided them for their unbelief and hardness of heart, because they had not believed those who saw him after he had risen" (Mk 16:14).

The catechesis of Christ has a strength which distinguishes it from any coarse didacticism; this cannot be said of any other teacher in human discourse. It can only be due to his being both teacher and the teaching, in a fusion that not even the great Buddha or Mohammed or Confucius claimed. If Jesus Christ is but a partner of the Law Giver and the Prophet, it would suffice to name high schools after him, and leave it at that. If he is the hero without the combat of the cross, then he should have a teenage fan club, and leave it at that. If he is only another dead man on the cross, then he could be deserted at every sunset on each Emmaus road. Christ the Living Word is his own answer. As a character in a Bergman film says: "If one can believe in God, there is no problem. If one cannot, there is no solution."

Misguided theology has a problem but does not confront it; it pretends to be the solution, and gets wrapped in the contemplation of contemplation. Whatever form of error it chooses to take, it trips over its own syllogisms. In 1870, for example, as Pius IX solemnly defined papal infallibility, the Vatican was shaken by the fiercest thunderstorm Rome had known in many years; an atheist said it was the voice of an angry God proving there was no God. In 1984, when the roof of York Minster Cathedral was struck by lightning after a controversial ceremony, a church official called it an act of Providence since the rest of the cathedral had not been struck. The commentary of God himself is more empirical for our benefit: "When it is evening you say: 'It will be fair weather for the sky is red.' And in the morning, 'It will be stormy today, for the sky is red and threatening.' You know how to interpret the appearance of the sky, but you cannot interpret the signs of the times" (Mt 16:2–3).

The signs of the times are read by people radicalized by the life of the virtues; for theology is a divine science done by humans and the virtues are the school of humanity. Theological science repays its debt to virtue by guiding children and men and women to sanctity. The idea has been called anti-intellectual by some who say theologians must not leave their brains at the door. But theologians must not leave their bodies and souls at the door either. In that case it would be fascinating to see what entered. God does not leave his brain at the door when he comes into history; he rather gets one for himself, who never needed one before. And the brain is with a body and soul; he is mind and heart, brain and body together when he is born and when he is killed. And he is brain and body when he passes through a shut door on the Day of Resurrection. That should affirm and enlist the intellectual vigor of the theologians to investigate holiness; but if they are less theological than they should be, the risen flesh and bones will be an affront to them. Having become habituated to trivializing every power and goodness to an "ism", the theologians who lose confidence in the highest virtues tend to dismiss triumphal holiness by snubbing it as "triumphalism". The words of one of the generals to Hannibal apply: *"Vincere scis; victoria uti nescis."* You know how to win; you do not know what to do with the victory.

The utter materiality of the Incarnation had the practical purpose of restoring holiness in history. This is why Christ was most practical about matters which seem impractical to the modern mind: before multiplying the loaves and the fishes, he looked around to see that there was grass for the people to sit on; amid the shouts when he raised the daughter of Jairus, he asked someone to get her a bite to eat; his own "hour" was timed to a precise clockwork which told him when it was not at hand and when it was; he catered his own farewell. Holiness is practical; indeed, it is the only kind of life that can be practiced well. The pagan patron of the synagogue got his compliment for being so practical; Jesus admired a man who knew what it meant to be "set under authority" and in that system to say "Go" and make a man go; and to say "Come" and have him come; and to say "Do this" and have it done. The victory of life is got by such practical simplicity; and it is only impractical to think that God does not operate according to some sort of causality. According to the pragmatism of the Upper Room, the apostles travelled the imperial world doing something purely and simply because the Man had said, "Do this."

Modern man has forgotten how the world works. That is a strange thing to say about the technical mentality; of course natural science knows more than it ever did about the works of the world, and how each working works. But as this information increases, the memory of how the works work together fades. This does not have to be; given the corporal attentions of God, it is not supposed to be. But it is so, because modernity divorced holiness from its other sciences and by so doing cut off the why of the world from the way of the world. The way the world works is simply answered: "I am the way" (Jn 14:6). But that is simple only by knowing why he is the way. If we begin with any other premise, we end up with every answer but the true one. That was the modern mistake, summed up in the remarkable configuration of Tillich who said, "it is as atheistic to affirm the existence of God as it is to deny it."

The alternative to the doctrinal orthodoxy which I have called radicalism is not practical science, but superstition. It replaces spirituality with spiritualism. I think Tillich was superstitious so long as he believed what he said. And I think the apostles were superstitious too, at first. They were not simple fishermen who ended up with a fantastic fairy tale; they were complicated fishermen capable of any fantastic tale until the Resurrection made them pure and simple. If they had been simply scientific, they would have said, "There is Jesus walking on the water" and "Here is Jesus coming through a wall." I do not mean they would have been calm about it; they probably would have shouted. But if they had been simple and straightforward they would not have denied what their eyes saw. Instead, they turned an empirical observation into a wild opinion: "It is a ghost." Without faith in facts, people haunt themselves unduly. It was not a ghost; not on the water, and not in the Upper Room. And God is not a ghost today, either. But modernity has made him one because modernity is not scientific enough. Instead of saying, "There is God deciding the fates of men", modernity says, "There is Fate deciding the fates of men." Instead of seeing a child of God in the mirror, modernity looks and says, "There is Superman." And each time a voice absolves from sin and turns wine to Blood, modernity says, "It is a ghost." As the theologian helps lead the way to sanctity, the theology of the theologian says in various ways suitable to the times and to the hearer, but always true to fact: "A ghost does not have flesh and bones and you see I have" (Lk 24:39). When all is said and done, this is the real way the world works.

Tradition

Theology amplifies the sources of behavior by explaining the tradition of people who have behaved differently but who have believed the same thing: tax collectors, fishermen, musicians, North African historians, Roman lawyers, Greek engineers, Florentine draftsmen, French playwrights, Prussian physicists, the Viennese baker who invented the croissant, and three Portuguese children who saw their nation's angel and Christ's mother. The theologian may not appreciate all he finds; just as he may not enjoy the spectacular color of magenta or the heady perfume of boxwood or the euphonious accent of the Australian. But they impinge as items to be sorted out without being pulled apart. Tradition has been called the democracy of the dead for that reason; and because it has been rejected in our own time, we might also call modernism the tyranny of the living.

To think that traditionalism is inherently reactionary is not to understand it. Reactionaries and modernists do not understand it. They picture the sacred deposit of faith as a pile instead of a promise; the reactionary wants to wrap it up, the modernist wants to blow it up. But the traditionalist trusts the development of thought; he treats it as neither treason nor rebellion. Orthodoxy is traditional because it confidently follows doctrine where it leads. Heterodoxy, whether in the style of integrism or modernism, is the propensity to make the truth heel on man's leash and stop when man wants to rest, like Peter in his ill-thought moment trying to stop Christ on the road to Jerusalem. The bold thinkers have known that the Hound of Heaven is not a lap dog; wise men have found him with rough beasts in a stable, and without even a foxhole in which to sleep.

Attempts to domesticate Truth use definitions that simply

do not apply. The tendency to label orthodoxy as conservativism, and modernism as liberalism, is an example. It does not explain what it wants to explain; it only gives a wrong impression of the facts. Political conservatives for the most part have functioned outside Catholic life; and modernists have shown a marked illiberality in dealing with people who hold Catholic doctrines. Political terms convey nothing to theology; and when they are stuck on as labels, they contradict what they are labelling. "Conservative Catholicism" as a title is unhealthy, the way "white Anglo-Saxonism" when described that way usually is racist; and anything that calls itself "Liberal Catholicism" is as self-conscious and suspect as a government that calls itself a People's Republic.

The Lutheran theologian Jaroslav Pelikan has a book, not free of defect, with an excellent title: *The Vindication of Tradition.* Tradition is the most radical object for any vindicator. The Redeemer is the Vindicator of the holy tradition, the Hebrew "Go-el" who ransoms a remnant of the tribe. Job was sustained by the conviction of a Redeemer who would live, even while his shallow companions advised him to get accustomed to his oppressive solitude. His information was limited, and he did not understand that the authentic Redeemer would live after having been killed, but Job held fast to the tribal confidence in redemption as a fact. Thus he embodied the Old Testament's great exposition of philosophical theology. He was more advanced than his cynical friends deliberately because of his obedience to tradition.

Contemporary theologians have this advantage over Job: they live on the developed side of Resurrection doctrine. Christian theology is witness to the Resurrection; so it is both a form of prayer and an apostolate, just as Job's theology was prayer and anticipation. There are no political views of the Resurrection, for to be liberal or conservative about the Resurrection is like being liberal or conservative about sunstroke. But there is one vast and inclusive Resurrection view of politics, which is why social, economic and political life has to be shaped in response to it. Because of this witness, the Church's authentic theologians are the bishops who have the initiative in each local church to proclaim the Paschal mystery. This is a very radical idea, but only because of its dramatic source in the breath of Christ himself. Theologians accredited by the Church help the bishops, as the presbyteral college assists the episcopal college at the altar: the idea of a "double magisterium" of bishops and theologians is as misleading as the notion that two priestly orders mean a "double priesthood". And the historicity of the theological task requires an even more radical principle, one quite unique among the mental sciences: the worth of any teaching comes not from its originality or from its astuteness or from its plausibility apart from the apostolic succession.

Three Myths Modernized

The human elements in the tradition of culture are the intellect, the imagination, and the will. They have been challenged and denied in the modern age by the three disruptions of the radical tradition, modern in their expression but ancient in their mythic roots in rootlessness. Each, in the manner of Job's friends, considered the plaintiff voice to be the definitive voice, even when Job foresaw his definition in a Redeemer. Together, they have formed a modern culture which Georges Bernanos called a conspiracy against man.

The first mythic form offered to replace the persistent information about Paradise with an ethic of race and imminent power; this is the Promethean boast, realized historically in Satan's temptation of Christ to soar from the pinnacle of the

Temple. The second replaces the dialogue of grace and nature with the impulses of the subconscious; this is the Narcissus myth, shattered when Christ refused to worship the antithesis of love. The third rejects the spiritual combat as the tenable explanation of history and fabricates an economic dialectic; this is the Midas myth which Christ ridiculed when he refused to turn stones into bread.

Each persists in its claim, after having failed to find root in fact. The important work of theology now is to learn from their void. Racism and physical power have taken whole nations down in a flaming lake of sorrow. The beguilement of psychological contempt for transcendent moral demands has only riddled the world with unbridled neuroses. The social unity of history without a spirituality sovereign to history has cracked open the most violent cataract of disorder and carnage in history.

The mood of shallowness, which thought these myths were the dew of the new dawn, is a melancholy weariness. It would seem that Satan has been given a second chance to quote Scripture in the wild land. Geneticists who fear the unruly population of the planet wearily deny the awful fact: rejection of the sacred tradition has caused the death of more men and women in the last fifty years than the sum killed in all the centuries since hammers fell on Actium. Determinists glance stonily upon the hoards of refugees from the paper paradises of socialism. Clinical analysts turn their ears from colleagues who have found archetypes and values truer than lust.

An archbishop recently gave a speech on the dignity of life in which he said, "We are not trash. God is not finished with us yet." A reporter asked a bystander, "What did that mean?" His perplexity, if you will, comes from having absorbed a thing noxious as bad air. Theology, as theology, rescues thought from such a neurosis of alienation, a neurosis caused by thinking lightly about too many deep things. The neurotic element is an attitude toward empiricism which makes empiricism everything, as if it meant the same as an empire. Mental jingoism is not nobler than any other kind. It is probably worse. It plants its flag in places it has not even yet discovered. Fifty years ago, the positivist Schlick claimed, " . . . in principle there are no limits to our knowledge. The boundaries which must be acknowledged are of empirical nature and therefore never ultimate; they can be pushed back further and further; there is no unfathomable mystery in the world." The imperial "Scramble for Africa" was weak tea compared with this empirical Scramble for Everything.

A fathomable mystery is only a marvel; there are things more marvellous, and these are the things which are unfathomable. To suppose otherwise, is to believe the seminal Promethean myth of the superman for whom unfathomable things are merely things that have not been fathomed yet. The idea is impossible because supermen are impossible; but unfathomable mysteries do exist, and so saints exist, in sublime refutation of the superman. Saints are not only possible, they are expected: sanctity is the purpose of human life, for human life is a capacity for God. Without God, humans do not return to flesh, but to dust. Materialist anthropology, or shallow radicalism, fails to realize the significance of the flesh as it is implicated in history, because it denies the existence of eternity. By the promise of eternity, the human appetites can be ordered according to inspired intelligence and will. But modern analysis rejects this solution to alienation, as did the disputers of the synagogue in Capernaum who walked away from Christ. The Good Physician diagnoses the cases of egoism in each secular myth, and the alienated soul will not tolerate the biopsy.

Pride and Humility

Pride is the deliberate denial of radical truth. Without the realism of humility, the individual and possibly the culture succumb to one of pride's two extremes. These are sentimentalism and rigorism. The unique unhappiness of modern alienation combines them: the alienated modern has lost his shame but not his guilt. The modern figure is a sensual puritan. Among the aberrations in theology, the theory most typical of this is gnosticism. It distorts the relationship between truth and circumstance, between philosophy and history. It is a good camouflage for any escape from reality. Gnosticism detours words from their indications and incants them as though they were real in themselves. Hence its love of slogans. It tries to make of words what only the divine Word could make of himself; it tries to incarnate everything except the Incarnation, grasping at ghosts instead of God. Since that is impossible, it treats anything as an abstraction. The modern ideologue, who is a rampant gnostic, can cope with any problem except a real one.

In valid theological discourse, the terminology is unsentimental. But gnosticism can sentimentalize it, and does so to alleviate the burden of guilt. When, for instance, the Holy Spirit is consistently referred to only as "Spirit", when the Church is "Church", and the economy of grace is a "process", then you may be up against the jargon of gnostic ideology. It is quite specific about the need to be unspecific. Why has the definite article been dropped from a definite thing? Which Spirit is meant? If "Church" is the same as the Church, why use a pedantic Hellenism? The theologian of probity knows that spirits other than the holy One are legion, and that many churches have come and gone but only One remains forever. And if process replaces procession, is it because there is nothing conclusive to process toward?

The modern problem has affinities with the fourteenth-century nominalists who separated heavenly and earthly systems of reference. While gnosticism is far older than nominalism, the nominalist disruption of intellectual unity gave a new impetus to the confusion between history and revelation. The Church, for example, has recently encouraged and amplified the ancient concept of herself as the People of God, but is satisfied with it only in company with the description of the Body of Christ. That places historical experience above the communal sentimentalism which is a nominalist conceit. Separate faith from fact, and any sort of false character can be ascribed to the Church. The myth of the Church as independent of historical revelation refashions the Body of Christ into whatever sort of body one wants it to be. And at the same time it casts aside the temporal facts of the Church as though they were impediments to a higher plane. Thus the "institutional Church" is thought to be innately defective, not part of the spiritual plan, and an impediment to a nobler design. The modernist ecclesiology which holds this is as unrealistic as the idealizations of the nominalist Occam six hundred years ago. Occam, for instance, sounds much like a modern progressivist as he sides with the strictest poverty of the "Spiritual" Franciscans against the cautions of John XXII; it is an example of how sentimentalism and rigorism combine to reject the Church's common sense. Yves Congar described some of the consequences then which have not changed these many centuries: "... consciences became shaken, the certitudes concerning the Church's structure, the role and powers of the hierarchy started to dissolve; there began the dissociation between the institutional Church and a pure Church of the true faithful: the theology of the sacraments was questioned; and people showed inability to think of the Church as a sacramental organism".

Lower human nature, even when motivated by ideals, may get used to inferior descriptions of the Body of Christ. But there is little permanent solace in them. And in a pragmatic sense, they just do not work. The soul is not meant to be anonymous, or to remain unassimilated in the vital tradition of salvation history. It can only find its place through the matrix of the historic Church which is the transmission of that tradition. The one possible alternative is to be assimilated by the world as a particle of reality; the populist calls this solidarity with humanity; but this is unsatisfactory, since humanity is a figure of speech. God did not create humanity; he created humans. Society has no virtue; men and women have virtue in society. And history is neither a chronicle nor an autonomous dialectic; it is a conversation, indeed a song, between Perfect Love and his imperfect but perfectable object.

Liberation Theology

There is something sympathetic in the young Marx's attempt to deal with alienation, his *Entfremdung,* as the central human problem in terms of purposelessness; and there is much that is pathetic in the decision of his later years to replace that with economic exploitation as the definitive calamity. In this he was like the young romantic, willing to die for his beloved, but who soon enough becomes enamored of anything that can save his life. It is the degenerative psychology of every heroic heretic. In this, he resembles as much as anyone the young rebel of the mid-twentieth century who soon rebels against his rebellion; he cuts his hair and finishes school, but then looks to money to numb his servile guilt. After all, the Marxist and the plutocrat are both failed radicals; one takes up the myth of the worker and the other the myth of the manager, but both do it to avoid the radical fact of God.

Certain forms of liberation theology try the same shallow radicalism. The concept of liberation is theological, and Pope John Paul told the Brazilian bishops: "When purified of elements which can adulterate it, with grave consequences for the faith, this theology is not only orthodox but necessary." The elements referred to are those which appropriate Marxist economic dialectic to structure a new kind of Christian hermeneutic. Marx knew, and said, that his derivative Hegelianism was incompatible with Christianity. Elaborating on Feuerbach, he found religion an inadequate solution to the central modern problem which he had first identified as separation from a sense of purpose. Religion was a pathology for Freud; it was an inadequate philosophical myth for Marx. But he meant that a new myth was needed and, as with Judaeo-Christian consciousness, it would have to explain history. I have named the myth essentially Midan because of its utopian expectation of a materialist solution which ends up only complicating the problem. But it is as much the synthesis of all modern myths, quite as Pius X called theological modernism the synthesis of all heresies: Narcissistic in its oblivion to the social objectivity of transcendent love; and Promethean in its contempt for humility, enabling Marx without trepidation to call Prometheus "the noblest of saints and martyrs in the calendar of philosophy". That is equivalent to calling Adam the noblest of saints and martyrs in the calendar of religion; for the Christian, he is the essential adulteration of theological truth. So in a sense Marxism is best understood as a superstitious chiliasm—and also as the deadliest form of it.

Marx insisted that, according to the dialectical critique, theories be judged by their application; by its own analysis, then, Marxist dialectic disproves itself. After some thirty years in control of three-quarters of the world's nations, Marxism has been an unmitigated failure economically, culturally, and morally. The more words are written to defend it, the more they cancel themselves; the ideological dialectician is like the squid in a Spanish recipe, cooked in his own ink.

There are few Marxists in Moscow. Unreconstructed Marxist-Leninists are as rare as unrevised Freudians. There would be nearly none at all, were it not for some Christians who try to apply the dialectic, as though the strength of a symbol vitiated the burden of a fact. But by appropriating Marxist critique, theology ceases to be theological and becomes ideological. The Latin American liberationist, Gustavo Gutierrez, says: "Nothing remains beyond political commitment." The ominous meaning of this, as Cardinal Ratzinger puts it, is that orthopraxis is the only orthodoxy. The method of analysis is the conclusion of the analysis; or, the manner is the message. And the orthopraxis consists in the resolution of conflict. Even among orthodox Catholics, the fallout from dialecticism abounds: it helps explain the clerical tendency to reduce antithetical concepts to "leftist" and "rightist" labels and then to synthesize them to a middle position, a bland theosophy. The clerical form of dialecticism is called the "pastoral" approach; but there is little that is pastoral about it, if one knows what a shepherd is supposed to do. Pastoral issues always are theological issues and they cannot be resolved by abandoning theology. Many clerics have been trained at the graduate level in sociology instead of theology and, with the best of wills, may find it hard to understand the implications of this "pastoral Hegelianism". The figures that do understand, of whom the Pope himself is the representative, are more sophisticated in their vision, and for that reason may confuse and even threaten the clerical mentality.

The divinity of Jesus is an obstacle to Marxist orthopraxis as it contradicts the dynamic of class struggle; and so extreme forms of liberation theology reject it. They are quite less willing to tolerate Christological subtleties than were the schools of Bultmann and Heidegger. Ontology itself is reduced to one scheme. Gutierrez says: "The class struggle is an absolute fact and neutrality on this question is absolutely impossible." Our Lord's commentary on the salvation of the rich, that all things are possible with God, is rejected as "false universalism". Faith is cooperation with the dialectic; hope is confidence in the conflict; love is the synthesis.

The worker had been idealized by the clerical Fenelon and Lamennais long before, and by the disciple of Saint-Simon, Leroux, and by the Christian socialists of the Social Gospel movement in our own country. But in a way they could not have imagined, the attempt to Christianize the Marxist dialectic combines the troublesome complexes of sentimentalism and rigorism in a veritable nightmare. The Marxist liberation theologian is the quintessential "sensual Puritan". Confused in the analysis of nature and grace, he makes the "preferential option for the poor" an exclusive fact, and every theological doctrine is held accountable to it: the poor are pious for being poor in a reversal of Christ's beatitude in which the pious are poor for being pious; the Kingdom of God is an earthly convention, and the Eucharist is an allegory of the class struggle. When the Pelagian heretic known to us as the "Sicilian Briton" had written that rich men cannot enter the Kingdom of Heaven, St. Augustine wrote a famous letter in 414 in which he cited the parable of Dives and Lazarus as proof that the problem of alienation is not wealth, but the attachments and selfishness which wealth can, but need not, engender. But this makes no impact on the dialecticist who has a Pelagianism of his own which he adds to his materialism-and-gnosticism-and-dualism-and-nominalism in the mythic synthesis. *Non in dialectica complacuit Deo salvum facere populum suum.*

Because of the passion of commitments, and the detestability of social injustice, theologians may become impatient with the subtlety which their work requires. But the wholesale appropriation of material analysis is bound to be futile, like elevating gravity. And it is so, not because of political considerations, but because of the total discord between philosophies of history. A churchman seemed not to understand this when he spoke at the University of Chicago to celebrate the Seventh Centenary of St. Thomas Aquinas; for he called on the audience to apply Marx as St. Thomas had applied Aristotle. It was a heady challenge; quite literally so, because the difference between what Aquinas had done and what this man was asking the audience to do, was the difference between a heart transplant and a head transplant.

The theologian who succumbs to the essential material error of the economic dialectic, empties theology of reality, rejects the transcendent character of the struggle between good and evil, and mythicizes the Resurrection. If the Church cannot be eradicated, it is to be appropriated; the charism of the hierarchical constitution is said to be an anti-proletarian bureaucracy; grace is a product and the sacraments its means of production; and the Church herself is reserved as a privilege of the Party *cognoscenti*. Of course, this is a transitional program. The "People's Church" in Nicaragua and the movement "Pax" among some Slavs are examples of Lenin's prescription: "To finish off religion, it is much more important to introduce the class struggle within the Church than to attack directly religion itself."

The impulse increases—and does not decrease—as the credibility of Marxism wanes. Cardinal König of Vienna has commented on the new anti-Christian combativeness of Soviet client-states, as they become impatient with the "slow death" of theism. A considerable number of the clergy and religious cooperate in a tragic paradox; the chiliasm of Marxist liberationism, while claiming to be anti-clerical, abolishes everything about the Church except clericalism. It exploits the clerical mentality by setting up a kind of secularized Caesaro-Papism. In the Soviet *Izvestia* (October 8, 1984), Dr. Kudachkin writes:

> In Nicaragua the Sandinista government has three Ministers who are clergymen—the Ministers of Foreign Affairs, Culture, and Education. The Vatican insists that they leave their posts, on the pretext that the Church should not interfere in politics. But they are marching together with the people and are fighting together in the name of the people's freedom and happiness.

What sort of Catholics would allow themselves to be appropriated in such a cynical way? If one does not impute malice, can it be that this is only the update of the "old modern" naiveté which trapped the minds of Joseph Davies, and Julian Huxley, and Eleanor Roosevelt on her blithe tour of the Gulag? While all forms of liberation theology are not condemned, that which is rejected is rejected for its cosmic unreality. Theology of liberation is not theological until it is theology of redemption. The preferential option for the poor should be more than a reflex; it must be a preferential love for the poor. As a tenet, this is hopelessly bourgeois and evasive to the "old modern" ideologue. Yet in the face of the challenge raised by liberationism, the theme of the "anti-Word", which has been a preoccupation of Karol Wojtyla as university professor and Pope, takes on new force in the Encyclical *Dominum et Vivificantem.* The human disobedience to God takes away the freedom to participate in truth and love and makes men and women naive instruments of the "father of lies". The Pope characteristically alludes to the Story of Creation; if the Church should someday declare John Paul II a Doctor of the Church, an artist could show what real radicalism is by painting him seated in the Chair of Peter with his finger pointing to the Book of Genesis.

> God the Creator is placed in a state of suspicion, indeed of accusation, in the mind of the creature. For the first time in human history there appears the perverse "genius of suspicion". He seeks to "falsify" Good itself, which precisely in the work of creation has manifested itself as the Good which gives in an inexpressible way: as *bonum diffusivum sui,* as creative love. . . . (n. 37)

This is what confounds the Marxist dialectic applied to theology. It lacks the philosophy to see the weakness of its analysis; and its metaphysics is inadequate to trace the lies of Prometheus and Narcissus and Midas against the Good.

> Man will be inclined to see in God primarily a limitation of himself, and not the source of his own freedom and the fullness of good. We see this confirmed in the modern age, when the atheistic ideologies seek to *root out religion* on the grounds that religion causes the radical "alienation" of man, as if man were dispossessed of his own humanity when, accepting the idea of God, he attributes to God what belongs to man, and exclusively to man! Hence a process of thought and historico-sociological practice in which the rejection of God has reached the point of declaring his "death". An absurdity, both in concept and expression. . . . The ideology of the "death of God" easily demonstrates in its effect that on the "theoretical and practical" levels it is the ideology of the "death of man".

We must assume that liberation theologians are motivated by an honest zeal for the social dimension of the Gospel in the name of Christ who fed the people before preaching to them. Their heightened language is better understood in the context of the dismal conditions in those parts of the world where human suffering has not been ameliorated by adventurism and pietism. Their grammar is directed at exploiters who pretend that external conformity to orthodox Catholic formulas makes their impassibility acceptable. But the problem is this: the diction of the scandalized liberationist is divine indignation, but divine indignation is disordered in creatures whose capacity is for human indignation: "Vengeance is mine, I will repay, saith the Lord" (Rom 12:19). The Word of all theology is God, but the words of the theologians are not God. That would be to mimic prophecy. Liberationist language is absurd when it alleges that the Church has had no social program or previous theological imperative for social reform; and it is destructive when it becomes attached to a dualism of proletariat and bourgeoisie, caricaturing the Christian alignment of history.

There was a point during the Second World War, in an essay of 1940, when Arnold Toynbee acknowledged that the only interpretation of history capable of making sense in such a time was that of Christianity centered in the Incarnation; he lapsed into pessimism, but he had repudiated the servile impression of determinism. But now some liberation theologians have succumbed to that very servility out of desperation in the face of evil. And in that servility, born of a suspicion that there are injustices too grievous for correction by grace, they lapse into the semi-Arianism of the Pelagians like the "Sicilian Briton", who in fact have been the most irresistible sirens of the bourgeoisie. It has to be said that the dialecticism of Marxist-oriented liberationists is phenomenally bourgeois through its romantic European sources. In their dispirited state they do an essentially European and romantic thing, and a thing decidedly anti-proletarian: they lash out at all that is Catholic and baroque. In the United States, too, support for them is in no little measure an intellectually respectable camouflage for anti-Romanism.

As Marxist critique has failed, so liberationism based on it is

committed to a failed revolution even before it begins. To
reject authentic salvation history as the matrix for social reform
is to end up with a false confidence. There is a sad spectre of
titanism about it which claims that it cannot sink even as it slips
into the sea. Even the European sources are losing interest;
certainly the most vital French philosophy is now rethinking
the established existentialist orthodoxies of the last generation.
An historic event may have happened in the short time
Solzhenitsyn spent in Paris at the start of his exile: one writer
said that his presence revealed to a young generation of French
intellectuals the superficiality of their existence. In a broader
way, the many recent conversions of Western intellectuals seem
to signal a refocusing on old assumptions. And not all of them
are young idealists. One thinks of Malcolm Muggeridge's profession of faith, and of the deathbed conversion of Kenneth
Clark who had distinguished himself to viewers of his television series "Civilization" with his erudite, congenial, and patronizing condescension to Catholic thought behind Catholic culture.

As with other thought processes thought to be true for
being modern, Marxist liberationism is simply inadequate to
the realities of post-modern life. The Catholic objects, then,
not to its radicalism, for it is not radical to the extent that it is
not Catholic; the Catholic must object to its bourgeois smugness.
Certain liberation theologians seem prepared to acknowledge
this. But when a theologian is an ideologue, and God becomes
only a cause, then such reflection is impossible.

I am arguing for the opposite of retreat from political facts:
human suffering is increased when it is removed from the
context of eschatological drama and is forced to fit a synthetic
anthropology. Man is too great to be squeezed into that. St.
Augustine called Christianity a sea in which elephants can
swim and a shallow pond in which lambs can paddle. I suppose
we could say that materialism provides a pond for elephants

and a sea for lambs. That certainly would describe a People's Church. The measureless dimensions of the Faith exist because it knows the height and depth of all things, good and evil above all else. "Our wrestling is not against flesh and blood, but against the principalities, against the powers, against the rulers of this darkness, against the spiritual hosts in high places" (Eph 6:12).

The definitive wrestling took place in the mystery of the Passion, for man in his suffering remains an "intangible mystery", and its resolution must also be a mystery: "And if one asks him, 'What are these wounds on your back?' he will say, 'The wounds I received in the house of my friends'" (Zech 13:6). The violence of the prophecies against false shepherds bespeaks a transcendent conflict; it is won only through the redemptive authority of Christ who returns in victory from the struggle still bearing his wounds. In the Marxist idiom, there is a contempt for the theology of the Cross, and the contempt is as gnostic in its attempt to "socialize" the struggle against evil as were the extreme allegorizers of the Protestant Revolution: Johannes Tauler and Thomas Müntzer. Social suffering is the result of an evil more portentous than the social oppression which is its material cause. It is manifest in man's oppression of man, but originates in Satan's oppression of the whole human race.

At the same time, this does not connote a dualist mentality in which the forces of good and evil are equal contenders. The spiritual combat of God and Satan was permitted by God in the economy of free will; and the oppression of Christ on the Cross was allowed by the kenotic humility of God in the Incarnation. It is often said that the *Magnificat* of Mary is the most revolutionary song in any literature; but it is prelude to the greatest hymn of struggle, the Reproaches from the Cross. These cannot be understood properly as revolutionary in a political sense, although their social consequences are vast beyond reckoning; Mary, no more than Hannah of old, and Christ, no more than Joshua of old, sang of a classless social order. The will of God transfigures the given order; if the mighty are cast from their seats, the seats remain and are filled by the humble and meek. Such is Redemption and it has a permanent character; while there are counter-Revolutions in the political order, there is no counter-Redemption. Redemption is the universal reference for all material reform, and confers the spiritual maturity to participate in the suffering of Christ. Suffering is only a capitulation for the materialist; for the Christian, it is a necessary element of salvation. Thus the extraordinary words of St. Raymond of Pennafort which must infinitely perplex the determinist:

> May you never be numbered among those whose house is peaceful, quiet and free from care; those who live out their days in prosperity and in the twinkling of an eye will go down to hell. Your purity of life, your devotion, deserve and call for a reward; because you are acceptable and pleasing to God your purity of life must be made purer still, by frequent buffetings, until you attain perfect sincerity of heart. If from time to time you feel the sword falling on you with double or treble force, this also should be seen as sheer joy and the mark of love.

Cruel arrogance could apply this to justify the oppressor of the oppressed in society; but it is a reminder of the metaphysical dimensions of suffering, and the merits obtained by mortification. As such it is a counsel to engage in a battle worth the dignity of the children of God. Only then can the soul countenance the full power of Christ's words: " . . . as you did it to one of the least of these my brethren, you did it to me." The radicalism of Catholic Christology provides the one practical way to raise the dignity of men without lowering the dignity of God. Collectivism as a solution loses sight of the right relationship between solidarity and subsidiarity; it becomes an evolutionary pantheism. And that may be one of the worst mistakes of some liberation thought: it makes the People of God into God and adapts the theological language of Exodus and Redemption to an obscure syncretism based on Hegel's definition of God as the "Idea which is eternally producing itself". The vagueness only increases the alienation it tried to cure, as when Bakunin virtually parodied the Christian Passion with the archetypal Marxist dictum, "To emancipate the masses of the people, it is necessary first to subjugate them."

Ideology

The thinking person, privileged with the affidavits of several generations' experience, is morally obliged to realism. One cannot afford to repeat the charades of Dean Johnson canonizing Stalin from the pulpit, Mrs. Webb raising a shrine to Lenin in her London sitting room, and the National Council of Churches deputation reporting back from a trip to Moscow in 1956 that "there seems to be no interference with worship in the church". Whatever the social historian makes of this, it is not the theology of the innocent; it is very much the ideology of the ignorant. And its exactions in lives and torment have been beyond horror.

Theology simply ceases when it becomes ideology. A mistake, possibly the first mistake, of ideologues is not that they dwell exclusively in the realm of ideas. The opposite is the case: ideologues congregate everywhere but where ideas breathe free. In true gnostic fashion, ideologues call everything an idea except an idea. For one thing, they turn people into ideas of people. If the man is their idea of a man, he can do nothing wrong: his crimes are *faux pas;* his lies are witty; his stupidity is charmingly rustic. But if the man is not their idea of a man, he can do nothing right: his education is too frail or too fancy; his motives are too blatant or too byzantine; his moustache is too straggly or too stylish; and if he does not act superior, it is because he is inferior. Lurking behind the ideologues' critique is the conviction that God is their idea of God. Intellectual opponents, then, are inhuman enemies of the ineffable idea. There is no point to debate: the plan is to conquer. There was a time when debate was a way to make friends; it has become the opposite. The fiery Edwardian debates followed by a round of spiked punch have become anemic "dialogues" followed by a round of spiked punches. And when liberationism becomes ideological, it not only shuts down debate, it then marches off to start its own idea of a church.

The whole new set of modern manners can be corrected only by a radical rowdyism of the saints; holiness is the one effectual union of the person with the idea of the person. It is radical because it is acquainted with the Being behind being; and it is rowdy because it refuses to be domesticated. Attempts to revolutionize Christianity can only domesticate it to a set system. Of course Christianity is gloriously domestic and even has a Holy Family; and that is exactly what makes it so undomesticated and unfamiliar to the ideologue. Nazareth is Nazareth and not the idea of Nazareth. It is domesticity when God tabernacles with us; it is domestication when we redesign the tabernacle. Modernism redesigned it in various ways, but God refused to dwell there. He became man, but he did not become our idea of man. And that was the most providential of acts; for it preserved the right proportions of man and of history. In a domesticated Christianity, greatness seems merely gigantic, and the saints brood larger than life. Only by ortho- doxy are saints saved from gigantism, to become the perfect models of normalcy. Ideology pretending to be theology makes it easy to be big and impossible to be great. It makes Christianity larger than life when it is meant to be as large as life was when Christ lived it. Only the one, holy, catholic, and apostolic Church cannot be outgrown; only her creeds can outfit a soul. She is called Mother, not a Movement, for she knows maternally how to handle souls without undoing them. She binds them to no system other than grace; she teaches them no dialectic other than a psalm; and then she lets them loose in an idiosyncratic world where their most agreeable affinities strike the ideologues as grotesque: the fasting reveller, the celibate lover, the urbane hermit, the candid diplomat, the married virgin, the honest lawyer, the practical mystic, the gentle soldier, the poor physician, the modest beauty, the humble king.

The Holy Vision

I cannot think that I have suitably examined any of the critical issues in modern theological debate; an essay can only try to identify what some of them may be. The conclusion, if there is to be one, is this: true theology is radical, but it will seem placid and even timid to a point of view which has a limited concept of human sources. The limited view may seem to be a radical view, but only to itself. The authentic Christian adventure continues to be in the line of those who expose and confound attractions which are uglinesses ever new, ever ancient. The heroes will be those who are fed up with the pretensions of heroics: they will be like John Chrysostom, Peter Claver, Leo XIII, who challenge the pretensions of inadequate social science. Dorothy Sayers said that our successors will speak of the modern materialists with the same tone that modernists reserve for the Victorians: " . . . 'faith in the future' will seem to them as reprehensible as 'nostalgia for the past' seems to us; and their journalists will use 'twentieth century' as ours uses 'medieval' by way of a handy term for such crudities, cruelties and superstitions as they may happen to disprove."

When modern theologizing has been most shallow, it has been so as a lack of good philosophical and historical judgment. Better information would have shown that the new mistakes have antecedents in all the ages of Christian life: in the apostolic, primitive, imperial, mediaeval, divided, and secular. The name of the seventh age is unknown to us; but if the Christian philosophy of history holds fast in which the Lord of history disqualifies any Lordship of history, and voices are not mute that speak for it, the next age will not be named for the shallow radicals who have already failed to keep their appointment with history and their trust with the Being who governs it. And the friends of the poor then, as now, will be what they have been since the Truth became poor among us: the friends of God. Justice, democracy, and human dignity will not be arbitrary concepts, and the force of history will not be "God above God". The prophets will not be those who, in the words of the Salvadorean bishops, claim "for themselves a representativeness of the people they cannot certify in clear form". Popular fronts are popular for a while; but they are, after all, only fronts. They cannot hold back for long the wild calculations of the saints who estimate human worth to be more than something worthwhile, and find it to be a thing worth everything.

The holy vision refutes any depiction of the virtues as bourgeois conventions by practicing them extravagantly in every social order. Without the vision of grace, capitalism, which is morally neutral, can become as anti-social as communism. Peace, justice, and prosperity are fantasies without the righteousness of revelation. If such fantasies were believed really and widely, it would be the first time that a people long used to drawing truths from myths, had drawn a myth from the Truth. But there is no "God above God" for there is no "God beneath God". Nothing is God but God, and the theologian who can solve the problem of alienation is any man, woman, or child who knows that.

> He shall not judge by what his eyes see,
>   or decide by what his ears hear;
> but with righteousness he shall judge the poor,
>   and decide with equity for the meek of the earth;
> and he shall smite the earth with the rod of his mouth,
>   and with the breath of his lips he shall slay the wicked.
> Righteousness shall be the girdle of his waist,
>   and faithfulness the girdle of his loins (Is 11:3b–5).

VIII

POST–MODERN EVANGELISM

The world's leading evangelist is a Catholic, and were not the fact already becoming commonplace, it might seem incongruous to find that he is the Pope. John Paul II has been heard by more people than have all the evangelists from St. Dominic and St. Philip Neri to John Wesley and Billy Sunday. The parallel is not irrelevant and I trust not irreverent: by modern means, populations who may have entered churches as infrequently as concert halls are having their first encounters with bishops. And yet the Pope is almost always said to be speaking, not evangelizing, as if the concept of a Pope as evangelist is inconceivable. This certainly runs counter to the Pope's own enthusiasm for the word, and Vatican II's teaching that evangelism is the prime office of a bishop.

Dominic and Philip are properly called evangelists for it is a historic Catholic word. Only by default has it become some sort of popular antonym for Catholics. The Pope's general audiences have become veritable evangelical rallies; but in St. Peter's Square, when the resounding hymns end and the sick have been carried forward, there is heard a Gospel shorn of the cant and vulgarity which have become the media dress of pop evangelism.

If the evangelism is whole and effective, the Church should expect converts. In an allocution on Cardinal Newman in 1979, John Paul II said: "The Church must be prepared for converts." But to the present generation of Catholics in America the idea is almost novel. Thirty years ago in the United States there were 4.25 converts for every thousand practising Catholics;

today there are 1.25. Conversions dropped from 146,212 in 1959 to 88,000 in 1985. Some Catholics even seem surprised that in these restless years anyone should want to become a Roman Catholic. In some quarters the suggestion is practically rude; the word "convert", like the title "preacher", is so indelicate as to warrant a euphemism, like calling a leg a limb. Where Catholicism has been taken for granted, it has become anonymous; and where it was considered to be a reactionary social element, it has become positively actionary: by way of example, the loss of faith in many Catholic universities contrasts ironically with the growing phenomenon of conversion to Catholicism on the old and ivied campuses which once were the domain of the non-Catholic social establishment. As Catholics become more needful of interior conversion themselves, they grow more uncomfortable with any distinctive Catholic identity; and at the same time, some of the youth and intellectuals whom they sought to cajole are becoming vociferous about their newly discovered Catholic apologetics. The modern expectations are being turned around, or rather turned quite upside down: Catholicism is in decline only in the places which never expected it to decline, while her cultured despisers seem increasingly beguiled by her lure; the clerical mentality is more and more impatient with the vital demands of religion while the laity want their priests to show more priestly vitality, so that anti-clericalism has shifted from the laity to the clerics; and with profound consequence for the future of the West, the mission lands of the so-called Third World are beginning to send missionaries to the old Catholic lands.

Catholicism in the post-modern age will be more like the radical primitivism which the moderns claimed to seek but which slipped through their fingers. Primitivism is far from crudeness, but the moderns did think of it as a romantic feebleness and indefiniteness; and that is why the modern attempts to revive primitive vibrance in religion confected a sham: what was supposed to be a renewed worship, in too many instances resembled the primitive liturgy about as much as an Edwardian *tableau vivant* brought back Agincourt. Primitivism is a basicness of principles and a clearness of thought, a proximity to the sources; it is not a thing undressed, but a thing's first dress; it is not unceremonious, but ceremony unfaded, so that it is not grey but almost gaudy, a tiara of silver and stones instead of a homburg, a coat of arms instead of a credit card, a catacomb wall splashed like a rainbow and not a modern "worship space" in beige. It is anything but informal because it is the beginning of a form, and this is why the most basic man in a desert walks with a royal strut and not with a modern slouch. Primitivism has nothing like the vagueness and tentativeness of modern philosophy, for its lines of thought are as streamlined as a toga, as lucid as light working through an alabaster lattice, as blatant as a peacock that does not know the rules of self-effacement. If the Scriptures are primitive declarations, they are so in the sense that they begin by telling what happened in the beginning and end by describing what will happen in the end; there is nothing of modern "process" thought about this, because the Scriptures are the procession.

In whatever shape it tends to take, primitivism is a most threatening fact to a parochialism of thought that wants to live off the land instead of bringing life to the land. The rebelliousness of the 1960s and 1970s did not free the Church of parochialism; it in fact was an attempt to be nothing but parochial. In that, it was not a reaction against, but a bohemian variant of, the post-war "cute Catholicism" which muted the transcendent glory of the Church in order to show the amiable harmlessness of upwardly mobile Catholics. Neither the bourgeois nor the rebel anticipated the situation of today. To keep his sanity and heart, the priest above all others is going to have to address the deep questions being asked by people who have grown impatient with pedantic cheerfulness and aimless earnestness. The Catholic preacher is no longer addressing a completely modern congregation; if he proclaims himself a modernizer, he will look like an artifact to the post-modern eyes staring at him. If he does not accept this fact, he may have to withdraw and continue to celebrate modern folk masses for the elderly whose guitars have become a curiosity to the young.

Relativism

Awkwardness about conversion is to a degree the result of a misconception. The ecumenical imperative of Vatican II was popularized by the modern synthesis into a form of relativism: religions become subjective equations whose validity is not determined by revealed truths and reason but by the emotional solace which they offer the believer. Having discovered that elms and light bend, the modernist supposed that thought might bend, too. The one constant seemed to be that if it is not right to be right, it is at least good to be good. The background was the Western liberal penchant for moralizing. Applied to comparative religion, the justification of the Judaeo-Christian worldview comes to be its relevance for the moral life, apart from its dogmatic formulations. So, for instance, Mormonism or a mushroom cult may be commended on the grounds that its devotees have a substantial regard for old-fashioned family virtues. The Old Time Religion need then be no older than America and the Rock of its foundation would be somewhere around Plymouth.

The pervasive moralism of the West has so thoroughly posited hypocrisy as the only heterodoxy, that Catholics have to come to think it almost wrong to speak of conversion, frequently counseling prospective converts to "stay where they are" and strive for unity within their own traditions. It is a patronizing attitude, and it is counsel that would have denied the United States its first native saint. If Mother Seton was the guileless victim of imperial evangelists adding notches to their guns, so then were the fishermen on the Galilean beach and any Mohawk who met a Jesuit.

The Church's evangelism respects the independent disposition of individuals and perceives the gifts of the Holy Spirit evidenced in other communions. But the Second Vatican Council was qualified to grant these observations because it was in obedience to the Chair of Peter which, in the Council's own words, remains peculiarly entrusted with the full deposit of revelation. That this latter teaching has been left widely untaught is a token of the disparity between the Council itself and the amorphous entity, conjured by an obliviousness to the Conciliar documents, called the Spirit-of-the-Council. The plain fact is that the only Spirit of the Council was the Holy Spirit who is mightier than a bundle of good wishes and whose voice should distract any dancing at the foot of Sinai.

Shinto Catholicism

There is another factor stimulating the confusion of Catholics about the work of an evangelist, even when they agree in their estimation of its merits. I am speaking of ease in Zion. Quite apparently, Catholics have grown comfortable in modern America. After generations of life floridly complexioned by the nineteenth-century immigrations, the immigrant status has largely shifted but the complex lingers. This imposes on Catholics an imperative to assimilate and become accepted, a repetition of the odyssey into Canaan where the Hebrews deserted the Covenant for the "high places". A cynical society requires that the price of this adjustment be the sacrifice of Catholic identity, quite as syncretism became the passport into Canaan. The secular humanist will permit Catholics their "colorful traditions" with the largesse of the Department of the Interior underwriting a rain dance, but the universal commitments of Catholicism, such as Petrine obedience and educational philosophies contrary to secular polity, are expected to be diluted; and to a large degree this has happened, as is witnessed by the similar attitudes on divorce and moral issues held by Catholics and non-Catholics alike. It has also been observed that affluent Catholics and those in positions of public trust, such as educators, legislators, and Religious, do not uniformly enjoy the social liabilities of a prophetic faith, and are most unlikely to evangelize to conversion.

For all their strengths which continue to enrich immeasurably the fabric of ecclesial life, the ethnic identifications of Catholicism in the New World imposed on it culturisms so vivid that they became confused with the Faith itself. Catholics have allowed sociologists, sometimes even Catholic sociologists, to perceive Catholicism as essentially a cultural and ancestral entity with religious appurtenances. For this shadow version of Roman Catholicism I propose the name "Shinto Catholicism". But to have been an immigrant is not necessarily to have been an apostle. To leave things behind is not necessarily to forsake things. To happen upon a new land is an indifferent matter; to go there to proclaim the Gospel is singularly different. In the Catholic history of America there were both those who felt they had arrived and those who felt they had been sent. It is the difference between flotsam and jetsam. We are now entering a period in which Catholics are obliged to choose which succession to follow.

This is because, with increasing clarity, certain trumpets are calling Catholics to make that perilous choice which has been required of those various past generations whose difficulties may not be desirable but whose fruitfulness in producing good Christians and even saints is enviable. The bolder the issues, the louder the trumpets, and the issues today are so bold that they have a positively primitive ring: (1) Is it right to kill babies? (2) Should there be families? (3) Is Jesus divine? (4) Is there a resurrection of the dead? They are the very questions which occur to the editors of *Time* magazine as they did to Theophilus, and they are debated even in the seminaries with the same fascination, if not always the same semantic precision, as back on Mars Hill. Because they are deep questions, Catholics may find themselves embarrassed, doubly embarrassed because we are required to loosen tongues which years ago atrophied at the theological dialect needed today; and we have to use minds which in this generation have been fed some thin substitutes for dogma. And there is added that ironical self-consciousness of size; for the Catholic Church in America is so massive in her temporalities that she sometimes feels encumbered, like an exceedingly tall person who stoops in the knowledge that a lumbering giant is picked on more than an entertaining dwarf. But God did not multiply the Church without intending to use her scale as his unsurpassed vehicle for proclaiming his truth to all peoples.

Conversion as a Grace

Catholics in America have a claim of course in the hope of providence, so long as they really accept what Christ told Peter. But they will be sorely tempted against hope, much as were the "old Catholics" of England in the Victorian age.

Proud of Norfolk but weary of the fires of Tyburn, venerating the Tudor martyrs but cautious of any indiscretion which might make that example a precedent, they had secured a mild truce with the established order, a judicial division of Caesar's coin. Into that up-and-coming world walked the most eminent Victorian of them all. To the old Catholics comfortable with their accruing inheritance, John Henry Newman was as welcome as Banquo's ghost. For Newman was a visible presence reminding them that Catholicism is sufficiently precious to require pursuit and sufficiently elusive to require conversion. For those who had almost forgotten how they had been born, it was unsettling to encounter someone who had been born again. His very name is didactic. And when the new man came speaking newly of old truths, it was as disconcerting as being dragged into the delivery room when you had nearly convinced yourself that babies come from storks.

In Rome, Newman enjoyed generous hospitality as a Gulliver in Brobdingnagian drawing rooms, but back home across the channel he was bound in Lilliput. With one unbound hand he dipped an unfettered pen in his inexhaustible well of charity and wrote kindly of friend and foe, esteeming the merits of his former allegiance and his adopted Catholicism with elegant judiciousness; and when he laid down his pen forty-five years later, it is roughly estimated that his personal contact had converted 636 noblemen, 700 clergymen and 1100 of their children and wives, 700 professionals, 800 writers and artists, 612 young men who became priests, 164 young women who became nuns, besides the numberless workers to whom he devoted so much of his attention as teacher and confessor. And no English Catholic was held in higher regard by his Protestant friends.

Much of the reticence which he considered a weakness among English Catholics can be found today among U.S.

Catholics, and likewise there is a parallel in the enormous potential he sought to unleash. Most of all, he envisioned a challenge before the modern Church which is more present now. He described it in the famous "Biglietto Speech" of 1879:

> Hitherto, it has been considered that Religion alone, with its supernatural sanctions, was strong enough to secure submission of the masses of our population to law and order; now the Philosophers and Politicians are bent on satisfying this problem without the aid of Christianity. Instead of the Church's teaching authority and teaching, they would substitute first of all a universal and thoroughly secular education, calculated to bring home to every individual that to be orderly, industrious, and sober is his personal interest. Then, for great working principles to take the place of religion, for the use of the masses thus carefully educated, it provides—the broad fundamental ethical truths, of justice, benevolence, veracity, and the like; proved experience, and those natural laws which exist and act spontaneously in society, and in social matters, whether physical or psychological; for instance, in government, trade, finance, sanitary experiments, and the intercourse of nations. As to Religion, it is a private luxury, which a man may have if he will; but which of course he must pay for, and which he must not obtrude upon others, or indulge to their annoyance.

The new cardinal then expressed the confidence that this *apostasia,* while possibly the ruin of many souls, would be unable to do "aught of serious harm to the Word of God, to Holy Church, to our Almighty King, the Lion of Judah, Faithful and True, or to His Vicar on earth".

The evangelism of the present Vicar, and doubtless of his successors who will have access to even more efficient communications, promises more renewal of souls in the re-evangelization of the West than we can predict, and there is no warrant to expect this renewal to be confined to Roman Catholics: "The

Church must be prepared for converts." But in the same allocution, Pope John Paul added: "Converts must be prepared for the Church." Part of the preparation has to involve some anticipation of unfamiliar ways. For example, while there will be a welcome encounter with Catholicism's stunning universality and spontaneity of devotion, the convert may also encounter evidences of formalism coupled with a certain amount of laxity about authentic form; this can make the liturgy a stumbling block to the neophyte, even more than it has been for Catholics of liturgical sense. To mention this might be taken as a lack of confidence in the sources of liturgical renewal, which it is not; rather, it is a concern for the pedestrian abuses to which genuine renewal has been subject. The liturgy is normally the catechumen's most available sign of the Church's communal life as the Mystical Body of Christ, and so it is distressing to find it reduced in so many places to what Cardinal Ratzinger has called "rationalistic relativism, confusing claptrap and pastoral infantilism [which] . . . degrade the liturgy to the level of a parish tea party and the intelligibility of the popular newspaper."

The convert with visions of Solesmes and Chartres dancing in his head will need humility and prudence, which will be enhanced by the intercession of the Blessed Mother as model of these things, to disassociate the mystagogic from the romantic, and the ascetic from the aesthetic. None of these is out of place in Catholic life, but the sensible consolations of outward form are consolations only, and the soul needs to be encouraged with the knowledge of grace's insensible yet more objective working. While there is no excuse for worship done unworshipfully, the Holy Mysteries are confected by God through the utterance of the priests in the company of the people, and not by the diapason of an organ or the felicities of good speech. Or such at least has been the testimony of the catacombs.

"Meaningful liturgy" is meaningful only if it means something
to God; this is a lesson for both the enthusiast and the formalist.
One theologian observed some time ago:

> Perhaps [the convert] had nourished his spiritual life on the
> powerfully simple profundity of so many Evangelical hymns,
> and he must now live in a district where the Catholic hymn-
> book (sparingly and badly sung) is really much poorer in reli-
> gious substance. Perhaps he hungers for a word—a good Catholic
> word merely expounding the Council of Trent—on God's grace
> as justifying us sinners without any merit on our part, for an
> echo of the *"tu solus sanctus"* of the *Gloria* of the Mass, for an
> explanation of the *"per evangelica dicta deleantur nostra delicta"*
> which we pray every day, and he hears, in the only place where he
> can hear, perhaps, too many moral exhortations. The convert
> may easily be overtaken by a general feeling of homelessness. . . .
> He will comfort himself with the faithful consciousness that he
> had done what he had to do: to find Christ where he wants to
> be found, in His Church (*Theological Investigations,* III).

New Occasions Teach New Duties

It may be said with spare exaggeration that conversion is the
normative circumstance of daily life. In the light of the Gospel
it is almost eccentric to expect Catholicism to be something
got by birth. The Apostolic Faith is no more hereditary than is
the Apostolic Succession. A remarkable number of the par-
ables are about this, and they outrage social custom to make
the point: recall the Wedding Garment, the Prodigal Son, and
the Laborers in the Vineyard. The shining Teller of those
stories also spoke of being born again, and it betrays his trust to
let that phrase rust into a generic identification of a variety of
non-sacramental Christians. When asked by a man on the train,

"Are you saved?", a certain churchman replied: "Yes, but it was by such a very narrow squeak that I never boast about it." Being born again does not mean foaming about it, but it does mean realizing grace as a gift. The regeneration is expressed both as the baptizer asks sponsors to name a baby and, in a symbolic parallel, when a world of cardinals sits hushed in the Sistine Chapel to hear a new pope declare his new name. We are children by adoption. A lady once told me, in what I took to be a revealing slip of the tongue, that her parish had been in her family for three generations; it is how many may be inclined to view the whole Church Catholic. But the present time is too pressing to take anything for granted, and too demanding to make a possession of the Mystical Body which would possess every fiber of our being, body and soul, identity and commitment.

We are enjoying the reign of a pontiff who gives the age an impression that it is seeing the papacy for the first time. This surely is not because his predecessors had any lesser claim on venerability; perhaps it is because he is from an unlikely place or possibly because he has lived under a succession of deprivations and tyrannies expressive of all that has made the modern age such a tumult. As once in Judaea, this is not a work of subversion, but a fulfillment. Far from renouncing what Christ commissioned to Peter, he is reasserting it with a compelling voice; and if many reply with King Agrippa, "You almost persuade me", many others have become fully convinced, others whose only deterrent from Rome until now had been the papal claims. New occasions do teach new duties. And with the Papacy presiding assiduously in a world divided between dissent and inconsequence, an increasing number of thinkers are concluding that it is quite as contradictory to call the Pope "a great and good man who mistakenly believes himself to be the Vicar of Christ on earth" as it is to say that there walked through Galilee "a great and good man who mistakenly believed himself to be Christ on earth". If the Pope were so wrong about so weighty a matter, one should no more call him great and good than one should trust a senator who calls himself an artichoke.

I only mean to point out the oddness of the attitude. It is extremely odd, for instance, that claiming to be Napoleon is universally considered pathological, but claiming to be the infallible Vicar of Christ is dismissed as a theological indiscretion. Objectively, the latter claim is more daring, and practically it is more dangerous if it is not true since these days the Pope does have more divisions than Napoleon. But if it is true, it is a truth overwhelming all deterring sentiments of a secondary nature, be they affinities of taste, custom, or clan. There remain just two reasonable responses, and we may expect to encounter them with increasing volume: people either will grow closer to the Magisterium or they will grow more opposed. The middle way will shrink.

Surprised by Joy

This brings up the name of one of Christianity's great modern apologists who had the sense to see the superficiality of objections to Christianity exactly as they seemed to be sweeping the field of thought. The curious thing, though, is that C. S. Lewis, of whom I speak, impelled so many toward "Roman claims" which he did not fully embrace himself. So, in what I hope is not an unwarranted digression, I would consider his case briefly; for he does represent the noble kind of thinker who has a grasp on the wide scene of Christian truth and yet did not become a Catholic. As such, he represents the best in the sort of introspective mind at the demise of modernity, who has the right intuitions but labors under an intimidating weight of cultural baggage.

Roman Catholicism is not an aberration of, or addition to, a purer Christianity which faded with the Palestinians and Celts and survives only in a few university faculties; so it would be hard to say that Lewis stood for a core of non-sectarian authenticity with which various branches of Christianity can enrich their own identities. After all, to reject all denominations is to lay the cornerstone of a new one. And, when pressed to the point, Lewis did profess membership in a particular national church even as he clung to that element in it which he preferred to call deep rather than high.

His gracious demurral from party strife has made it easier for non-sacramental Christians to claim him for their own. On the other hand, it would be difficult to suggest that he is less useful to Catholic apologetic than to any other variety of Christian exposition. In fact, much of his apostolic and historic vision has to be edited to make him sound like a non-Catholic. To him as much as anyone does the casual reader of the twentieth century owe a debt for the clear expression of creation as a spiritual reality. His Screwtape let slip a sparkling insight of the sacramental economy when he complained of how God "made the pleasures: all our research so far has not enabled us to produce one." With light like this shining through his writing time and again, you might say that if Lewis could be declared a Doctor of the Church, it would well be under the title *Doctor Transfigurationis.*

One might also say, though, that he has impelled many along the "road not taken" by his not having taken it himself. If he rejected the deadly complacency of the *via media,* which has been called the last bastion of nothing much, he continued to let fall on himself the steady damp of the middle way. His unwillingness to abandon it is not necessarily a sign of either stability or stubbornness. One is welcome to the impression, however, that the pale elegance of the account of his conversion to Christian belief, *Surprised by Joy,* is a paraliturgy of the eucharistic feast which is Newman's *Apologia.*

It goes almost without saying that anyone who dismisses his glinting sentences as "precious" deserves the contempt of any fair critic. But the difference between Lewis and the Church Fathers might be made by giving him a designation of his own, something more representative of his personality and ecclesiastical role: not a Father of the Church but an Uncle of the Church. If it is time to bare souls, let me confess that there is a touch too much of pipesmoke and wainscote in Lewis and not enough incense and polychrome for people jaded by apocalypse. One so intent as this Church Uncle on the heavenly pilgrimage should have been less timid about travelling to great places. Only a channel lies between the Senior Common Room and the Sainte Chapelle, but Lewis, who made a supernatural science of homesickness for the Eternal City, made a natural phobia of seasickness.

I take this as a symbol of his dilemma, and if it is a romantic argument, well, Lewis provides the defense himself in his paramount ardor for honest romance. The romance was frustrated by not reaching all the way to Rome. But if his avuncular mien would not take up a Romish passport, he remained a friend to any Anglo-Saxon reckless enough to depart for degenerate and sultry climes. Not only was he benign at the parting, but in some sense he was a stowaway on board and a prescient literary guide when one got there.

He was so right in everything he said about the ritual of life, that he should have better understood the dangers as well as the benefits in ritualizing his own domestic benefactions. If he abhorred faddish curates redecorating chancels into less than the gates of heaven, he did not balance the excess by making the university faculty room a sacristy. The tweedy figure lighting his pipe can be as ikonic as Cyril swinging the censers of Carthage; and it will be remembered how that Father of the Church persisted in his axiom which our Uncle of the Church proposed but did not live to conclude: *Habere non potest Deum patrem qui ecclesiam non habet matrem.*

That the Church and not the University is universal is a thing he labored to say. Possibly Swift alone bested his craft in saying it so well. But why does he seem not only a don but positively donnish, when neither Newman, "that wreck of awful beauty", nor Aquinas, "the dumb ox", can fittingly be called that? And yet he is not "merely" (in his sense of that word's strength) so donnish as Ronald Knox, either. The power and ambiguity of his appeal to Catholics in this last modern moment may lie in this vagueness. Some Christian groups have made a point of fuzziness. But the Catholic must bear witness that ambiguity is not mystery; and docility toward the vague is not the same thing as docility toward the ineffable.

Lewis was amused to think of how his Ulster grandfather had looked forward to having civilized chats with St. Paul in heaven, unlike Dante who expected the apostles to be mountains. He sided with Dante in theory, but there may have been too much Ulster in him not to be wary of what effect a papal visit would have on the hedges around his own garden. If he is too domestic one way (Belfast *gemütlichkeit* iced by occasional Norse fancies and a little Latin sun), he is not domestic enough in another. His admirable village churches with rusticated crenellations are ever more Plato's cave of intimations than the domes of Solomon's holy place with their straight blasts of God.

Sir Richard Steele clarified a difference when he said that the Church of Rome professes to be infallible and the Church of England to be never in the wrong. A man like G. K.

Chesterton, who made it all the way to Rome, would have penned a limerick on the line; C. S. Lewis thoughtfully would have changed the subject. The phenomenon of the Church as sacrament is something of a lacuna in the Lewis books. But it is precisely this concept which saves belief from the gnosticism which Lewis objected to so keenly; and gnosticism will try to inflict itself upon the post-modern struggle to recover the soul of society, as the ephemeral ecclesiology of the gnostic has done constantly in times of social transition. The limitation in Lewis' apologetic style is not because he had no opportunity to digest Vatican II, although it is interesting to speculate whether he would have followed the post-conciliar course to Rome as have many other literary figures. But he had a grand enough picture of the Church to persuade others to follow the line of that vision to its source. He fired more imaginations than a stack of exhaustive treatises could; more people read C. S. Lewis than *Lumen Gentium* without warping their ecclesiology. This is a simple fact, and can only shock those experts who think families get up on Sunday morning and go to church in order to discover the identity of Proto-Mark.

The real explanation for the attitude of Lewis may lie in kingdoms rather than councils. For while the halcyon Lewis was a loyal servant of George VI, reverie imagines what he might have been, say, under Louis IX. And there is the romance again; it is not the kind of thing modern man would think about, but the age to come may ask it. Lewis right now, with his true face shining, might confess that all along he had wanted a gilded roof on Windsor and a king interested in the latest theory for refuting the Manicheans. But he did not have it that way; it may explain why he was surprised by joy while Albert the Great and Aquinas expected it. But having led so many young minds through a modern wilderness of brassy idols and hunger of soul, Lewis would well have been satisfied to think that he had a bit of a Mosaic part to play in deliverance; and if he could not be a Joshua crossing over into whatever follows the meanderings of modernity, at least he had gazed out upon a future which survives time and fashion.

Quo Vadis?

The Second Vatican Council spoke again, as the Church has been wont to speak in the most contrasting epochs of her life, of a supernatural love so expansive that it embraces all who would be embraced through contradiction. It was a promise and a pledge in the most critical moments of modern experience when people had begun to take abandonment for granted. But this was not an inconclusive testimony; for even in the midst of the modern age, the Church was pointing a prophetic finger toward the way of resolution. Tempered by a humility sprung from the knowledge that God chooses the foolish to confound the wise, the Church repeated the solid old claim that there is, and will be, warrant to expect all roads to lead to Rome. The post-modern situation may resemble the primitive in nothing so much as this: when one wants to hitch a ride there will be the tundrel of Peter and Paul and nothing else, for there are few imperial chariots in sight. Even St. Peter had second thoughts about the travel and in retreading his tracks he got the shock therapy of the *Quo vadis?* As Peter is the Vicar of Christ, so is he the type of the post-modern soul rediscovering its world and its God at the very moment it was fleeing from them. For wherever the line is to be drawn between modernity and whatever succeeds modernity, it will be at the place where modern man on the march grew abashed and exalted by a Voice rattling everything he assumed to be permanent, with the question: "Where are you going?"

Anyone who makes it to the last book of Revelation knows that the Voice is on a throne across a sea like glass; but at this moment in the history of culture he translates his *Quo vadis* as decisively as ever through a mortal man on a wooden chair across St. Peter's Square. There is not a shred of triumphalism in the sound, for it has matured through too much history to twist reality. But it is solemnly triumphant because it has seen the heart of history too close to deny it: "The Church must be prepared for converts and converts must be prepared for the Church."

IX

FREEDOM AND OBEDIENCE

Holiness is freedom functioning in the proper way. To be fully human, men and women have to obey the order established by God. Otherwise, disorder presents itself as a choice and the result is dehumanizing. This choice was made long ago by Adam and Eve, which is how there came to be original sin, or, that inherited part of the human condition which is not human because it is not free.

The long wail has wafted through history from all kinds of lips: "I couldn't help it . . . I just had to . . . I don't know why. . . . " Redemption means getting humanity back. It had to be done by Christ who was the one free enough to be truly human because he was also perfectly willing to do what he had to do, what his Father was asking of him. Pope John Paul II, in the apostolic exhortation *Redemptionis Donum,* repeated the first apostolic call to look to Christ who "redeemed humanity and made it holy by his obedience". Freedom is only true freedom, and not plain license, when it is subject to love; and love is authentic only when it is based on truth. Obedience, then, is fertile when treated as a matter of obligation; it is nothing less than the true way of loving (cf. *Imitation,* i, ix).

In psycho-social terms, if we are not obedient we are alienated. The refusal to obey is not liberation. And when alienation becomes permanent, it is, to use the appropriately ghastly word, damnation. Its dreadfulness to anyone with human sensibility lies in its concrete absurdity. By its Latin root, absurd means deaf; damnation is that fatal state of irreparable deafness to the voice of God calling the soul to be genuine to itself. Some of the current "liberation movements" may be discovering this inadvertently. For unless liberation from poverty becomes obedience to detachment, it becomes a form of possession by possessions; unless liberation from puritanism becomes obedience to purity, it will be an enslavement to lust; unless liberation from injustice becomes obedience to legitimate authority, it is anarchy.

There may be no more poignant indication of this sort of invention at the moment than the writing of the feminist Germaine Greer who now acknowledges that society is corroding because what she and others had called liberation from child-bearing has become a fear and hatred of children. "They promise them freedom, but they themselves are slaves of corruption; for whatever overcomes a man, to that he is enslaved" (2 Pet 2:19).

Without fidelity to the Source of Life, what is still called life is in fact a vacuum. What swallowed up the first Man and Woman has come close to swallowing the world. It begins with individuals and moves on to societies.

From the Book of Ruth we know what great thing happened to her when she told Naomi: "Whither thou goest I will go, thy people will be my people, and thy God my God" (Ruth 1:16). But we do not know what happened to the other woman, Orpah, who would not say it.

We know what was shown the docile thief who said to the Perfect Man in the middle: "Lord, remember me when you come into your kingdom" (Lk 23:42). But we do not know what the cynical thief saw as he shut his sad eyes at last. These are individuals. A large mass of souls alienated from their Creator institutionalizes that individual isolation in a new form for which there is a new name, totalitarianism.

Word and Anti-Word

The totalitarian mentality is a uniquely modern creation; its first use as a scientific category was by Mussolini. While tyrants of the past abused power which they claimed to have received from God, the modern totalitarian claims power as a substitute for a non-existent God. The loss of accountability amplifies willfulness, and willfulness on a grand scale opens the iron door to cruelty on a grand scale. The Psalmist prayed: "Harden not your hearts as in the provocation and as in the day of temptation in the wilderness." This desert becomes a mental wilderness barren of fulfilling human acts. Israel wandered forty years in the wilderness. Our Lord confronted aimlessness personified in the wilderness. Today, that confrontation has reached monumental social proportions and the wilderness has entered the human mind.

In Philadelphia in 1976, a relatively obscure figure stood up and spoke in a measured way about a great confrontation that was about to occur. The words were perhaps difficult to understand because of their ponderous style and depth of reference, and possibly unlike anything one comes across except in treatises of the mystics. It was not spoken of much in the aftermath of so many other activities which occupied the Eucharistic Congress. But the man had clearly made it his theme; he had said the same thing in a Lenten retreat to Pope Paul VI and the Papal household:

> When the devil says in the third chapter of Genesis, "your eyes would be opened and you would become like God", these words express the full range of temptation of mankind from the intention to set man against God to the extreme form it takes today. We could even say that in the first stage of human history this temptation was not only accepted but had not been fully formulated. But the time has now come. This aspect of the

devil's temptation has found the historical context that suits it. Perhaps we are experiencing the highest level of tension between the Word and the anti-Word in the whole of human history.

Having said it, the man went back to his own country, but he did not quite go away. Two years later, he appeared in white for the first time on the balcony of St. Peter's and told the people not to be afraid. Nor did the great theme go away, for it would occur many times in various expressions. Ten years after his Philadelphia address, in the Encyclical *Dominum et Vivificantem* (n.37), he writes in a passage from which one could build many essays:

> Man's disobedience, nevertheless, always means a *turning away from God,* and in a certain sense *the closing up* of human freedom in his regard. It also means a certain opening of this freedom—of the human mind and will—to the one who is the "father of lies". This act of conscious choice is not only "disobedience" but also involves a certain *consent to the motivation* which was contained in the first temptation to sin and which is unceasingly renewed during the whole history of man on earth: "For God knows that when you eat of it your eyes will be opened, and you will be like God, knowing good and evil."
>
> Here we find ourselves at the very center of what could be called the "anti-Word". That is to say, "the anti-truth". For *the truth about man* becomes *falsified: who man is* and what are *the insuperable limits* of his being and freedom. This "anti-truth" is possible because at the same time there is a complete *falsification* of the *truth about who God is.*

What is the "anti-Word"? That is hardly the way to put the question. Intelligence may inquire, Who is the Word? Then through reason and more than reason may be discerned the anti-Word. The Word says *"Serviam",* I will serve. And to the lasting agony of men and women upon the earth, the anti-Word says *"Non serviam."* The arrogation of the will to the self touches the human race and splits souls, pulling intellects and wills apart, with consequences in the moral order more devastating than the splitting of an atom in the physical order. These lines appear in a book: "In my hand a suitcase full of clothes and underwear. In my heart an indomitable will, I set out from Vienna." They seem harmless words until you read on the cover: *Mein Kampf.* Hitler's battle was against God. *Non serviam.* And those who do not believe in God still have not figured out how those two little words burned up half the world. They will not then understand how they burned up more than that. For the loss of one soul hurts the Word more than the desolation of a universe.

No Options

In the days of liturgical experimentation odd things occasionally happen. During an Easter Vigil, at the renewal of the baptismal promises, one priest referred the congregation to their paperback missals and intoned: "Do you reject Satan using Option Number One?" What is Option Number Two? Or Three for that matter? Of course there are no more options in regard to this question now than there ever were. No options at all in fact. Only a choice as Joshua gave it: "Choose this day whom you will serve" (Jos 24:15). And it remains the choice repeated by the new Joshua to his own men: "Will you also go away?" (Jn 6:67).

Here is not an arbitrary selection of moral attitudes. It is in fact a battle. St. Paul calls faith and love a breastplate and hope a helmet (1 Th 5:8), and opens an entire armory of virtue to equip the soul "against the world rulers of this present darkness"; truth, righteousness, the good news of peace, faith, salvation and the Word of God (Eph 6:10–17). St. Francis de Sales' spiritual mentor, Lorenzo Scupoli, entitled his guide to the interior life *The Spiritual Combat* and said that the combat requires four weapons: distrust of one's self, confidence in God, proper use of the faculties of body and mind, and prayer.

The moral conscience is an evaluative activity which can fight evil effectively only when it perceives harmony between the human person and the love of the good. Modernity rejected this connaturality, or ease of agreement, by rejecting the power of the absolute Good to forgive sin and by not trusting the Magisterium of the Church; only the Sacrament of Penance and conformity to the inspired tradition of the Church can give a sufficient spiritual instinct to the conscience. The truth about truth is that it is not a human invention but a gift which must be loved in order to be received. The heart of the spiritual battle consists in perfecting the will; for only by willing can one know, only by knowing can one love, and only by loving can one enter the full dimension of the truth.

As the struggle for perfection is the contradiction of absurdity, so the refusal to participate in the process of perfection forces the soul into a neurosis of disobedience. The alienated soul which hears Jesus say, "No one is good save my Father" (Mt 19:17), can barely hear his command, "Be perfect as your heavenly Father is perfect" (Mt 5:48). It is not a contradiction. Goodness is a natural moral characteristic based on fidelity to natural law and we can never get it completely right. Perfection is a state of grace based on fidelity to supernatural law. So we are not called to simple goodness, but to union with its source. As André Malraux expressed it, "Heaven is not a separation of right from wrong, but the apotheosis of the love of the good."

This then is what is meant by freedom: obeying the right purpose. Vatican II did not speak of the perfection of goodness; that does not exist. It did speak of the perfection of love, which in turn fosters goodness. Men and women do not become perfect by getting better; perfection happens when the soul yields to order. And there is no valid order that does not emanate from our Creator. Christ, the Perfect man, was such "through obedience" to his Father: "Thy will be done on earth as it is in Heaven." In his garden of obedience, striped with the light of divine humility and the sleeping shadow of human pride, he prayed: "Father, if it is your will, take this cup from me, yet not my will but thine be done." The Passion of Christ initiated the drama which would give ordinary people the ability to unite with Christ's obedience; that ability comes as a gift of the Holy Spirit. The Holy Spirit does not free individuals of the law; he becomes our law, so that we are bound to obey the truth as an act of love.

The Lonely Crowd

The combat between disobedience and its contradiction, begun in Eden and resolved in Gethsemane, is the solitary solution to the modern perplexity of people being alone together. Christ was not lonely, not even in solitude. Not even when his men deserted him. Not even when he wanted them to be with him. He was never completely alone. In the economy of the Holy Trinity, based on the supernatural obedience of love within himself, he said: "He who sent me is with me. He has not left me alone for I always do what is pleasing to him" (Jn 8:29).

The greatest spiritual combat day in and day out takes place in the confessional. The confessional is not a lounge. It is a battlefield. The experienced confessor knows that cynicism is a basic obstacle to the proper confession of sin. People have become so acquainted with infidelity in its many shapes and guises that they find it hard to believe in a perfect love which is truly faithful to them and their dignity. The cynicism may take the form of laxity on the one hand or of scrupulosity on the other. But it is a trick of the Prince of Pride.

A Sign of Futility

One even hears of confused modern souls who do not take recourse to priests but rather try to confess alone or to each other. What is this but a sign of futility bred of that insecurity which no longer trusts that we are genuinely lovable? Judas was not condemned for having betrayed God; others have done that, and one who did it three times became Pope. Judas entered the final pit of alienation for having repented "unto himself". You can see what happened: he abandoned providence for pagan fate. He broke obedience to the covenant which his people had freely made with God, and succumbed to the ancient notion of inescapable destiny, a kind of hellishness in which absurdity is the only sense and disorder is the one order. But Christ shattered that paganism by showing that the way to be free is to be obedient to freedom. Judas was not hateful. He was cynical. He thought he had to disobey. Therefore Christ said to him so sadly at their last common meal: "Go and do what you must" (Jn 13:27). Which means, in the courtesy of tragedy, "Go and do what you think you must." On that night of the betrayal of God by human compulsion, the whole tragedy of modern determinism was prefigured.

At the church where this writer works, there are two scents at Benediction: the incense at the altar and the marijuana out on the sidewalk. Catholic worship is the one efficacious proof against the cynical lie which claims drugs expand the mind while religion is the opiate of the masses. The fullness of truth in Catholicism is the unique guarantee that freedom is possible.

Those who rebelled against Catholicism first substituted a form of fatalism in the shape of predestination; in modern times they tried to level us all out under the gravel of determinism. But people who know how to adore God know how to overthrow such impositions: by submission to a grand obedience, after the model of Christ: "I lay down my life that I may take it up again. No one takes it from me, but I lay it down of my own accord" (Jn 10:17). And that is why the totalitarians strive to eradicate worship and kill holy people. They cannot tolerate souls freely submitting to a law which transcends all merely human decrees. They are totalitarian because in their bizarre system they demand obedience to their laws alone—an obedience to submission in place of a free submission to obedience.

Jacques Maritain said: "Authority and liberty are twin sisters who cannot do without each other, and authority in some is for liberty in others." Saint Irenaeus wrote from various angles to show how God gave us the potential to manipulate him so that we might be free to refuse to do it, and thus might we "become God by grace". But Satan only crudely says: "Disobey and you will become like God." Eve fell for that, losing her identity for the flashiness of a similitude, and so did one sad writer who recently published a new Magnificat: "Our souls magnify the holiness which dwells within us; yes, from this day forward, all generations will call us blessed; holy is our name." Centuries ago, some cults said the Mass backwards to invest divinity in the Devil; now this modern kind of theosophy, making perfect freedom a natural element rather than the gratuitousness of our Creator, incants the Song of the New Eve backward to invest divinity in the Devil's disobedience. We may come to look back on this deification of pride as quainter, though no less dangerous, than the way Utopians and Rationalists of an earlier age idolized the artifacts of pride.

To place a bull or a goddess of reason in a stone temple is extravagantly rude; but to enshrine the very principle of disintegration is cruder than rude, and clearly so when the shrine is of the latest synthetic plastics and smoothest chrome. There have been many such shrines in the twentieth century, and in them the dance around Calaban became a whirl around Chaos so suddenly that it was hard to get out.

If a darkening threat of confusion appears more imminent than the hint of an aurelian dawn, it is well to remember how our Lord asked those in Peter's tossing boat: "Why are you fearful, O you of little faith?" (Mt 8:26). He rose and rebuked the wind, and in that moment the calm became more commanding than the bluster: "What manner of Man is this that even the winds and sea obey him?" (Mt 8:37). Love is the one thing constant when a temper varies, and all because love is He; and what He is, He commands his friends to be. Thus Shakespeare:

> Let me not to the marriage of true minds
> Admit impediments, Love is not love
> Which alters when it alteration finds,
> Or bends with the remover to remove.
> O no, it is an ever-fixed mark
> That looks on tempests and is never shaken,
> It is the star to every wandring bark,
> Whose worth's unknown, although his height be taken.
> Love's not time's fool, though rosy lips and cheeks
> Within his bending sickle's compass come.
> Love alters not with his brief hours and weeks
> But bears it out even to the edge of doom.
>   If this be error and upon me proved,
>   I never writ, nor no man ever loved.

As so, in the power of the Holy Spirit one might add, nor then did Matthew, Mark, Luke, and John ever write, nor did Christ then ever love.

St. Peter went through the modern experience of disintegration. He said three times as Jesus was on trial by the savants: "I never knew the man" (Mt 26:72). But his speech betrayed him. And in the spare twilight of a century, modern man who thought he had come of age, wearing clothes too big for him, vestments as vast as eras and stoles as long as dynasties, opens his mouth and lets slip accents from the infancy of the world: beauty, truth, goodness, dignity, and virtue. The giants that once were in the land come back to lift him up. Their marathons still run their ways on his hard paved asphalt streets. Their spires still outsoar the chimneys of his gulags. Their gentlest words are still whispered furtively when men programmed with equations tell women rhymes about the moon. His speech betrays him.

In cities that have not died, thousands come on Ash Wednesday to hear the words: "Remember man, that dust thou art, and unto dust shalt thou return." Something makes them do it. In the midst of the glass office towers glistening with the suggestion that people might be robots without souls, there is a voice. More precisely, it is not a voice but eyes. Peter looked up after his third denial and saw them. Then he had to wait, for he could not go where Christ was going, not yet. His waiting on Saturday is the suspended anxiety of the modern age. The last days of the twentieth century are the Holy Saturday of human pause as Christ moves to harrow hell. Modern man thought he was doing it, freeing trapped things and brightening the dark. The existentialist thought he was doing it. The dialecticians, the fatalists, the psychiatrists thought they were unlocking the ancient vaults. But in fact Christ was doing it, for he alone knows how to call and be heard. Ego has no ears; Adam does. The sub-conscious has no ears; Lazarus does. Modern man has no ears; modern men do. Man can cancel God; men cannot: "Whither shall I go then from thy spirit? Or whither shall I go from thy presence? If I ascend up to heaven thou art there. If I make my bed in hell, behold thou art there also" (Ps 139:7–8).

God only requires that we remember our own names and that we be there with him, in whatever hell modern ingenuity invents and in whatever excellent moment it achieves. For all his failings, Peter obeyed a formed conscience which perceived that the most excellent moments, should they even include curing diseases and irrigating deserts and circling the earth, lead to little unless they lead to an eternity. After the muffled Saturday, when things seem obscured, came the clarion Sunday, and soon a voice: "Do you love me?" (Jn 21:15). This is how God teaches obedience to freedom. The Divine Authority always humbles and never humiliates.

Obedience and Love

Saint Thomas Aquinas said that obedience and love are one and the same, for love effects a union of wills (*S.Th.* II.II. q.114, a.3). Msgr. Josemaria Escrivá wrote: "Let us not forget that unity is a symptom of life. Disunion is decay, a sure sign of being a corpse." Looking back, we can begin to see how modern man fell apart as he lost the moral and spiritual unity of his culture. Only loyalty to the Chair of Peter, the seat of unity, can secure freedom of life and humaneness of humanity. It was hardly triumphalism, but an intuition of the genuine triumph of life, that inspired St. Catherine of Siena to call her pope, "sweet Christ on earth". Ecclesial attempts to fabricate "patriotic churches" without obedience to the real father inevitably splinter, whether in sixteenth-century England or twentieth-century China. Men must imitate Christ; men cannot duplicate him.

Pope John XXIII, in his diary (August 10–15, 1961), gave

an account of his mystical intuition of the majesty in this apostolic unity:

> After my first Mass over the tomb of St. Peter I felt the hands of the Holy Father Pius X laid on my head in a blessing full of good augury for me and for the priestly life I was just entering upon; and after more than half a century (fifty-seven years precisely) here are my own hands extended in a blessing for the Catholics, and not only the Catholics, of the whole world, in a gesture of universal fatherhood. I am successor to this same Pius X who has been proclaimed a saint, and I am still living in the same priestly service as he, his predecessors and his successors, all placed like St. Peter at the head of the whole Church of Christ, one, holy, Catholic, and apostolic.

Then the old Pontiff, whose own motto was *Oboedientia et Pax,* proceeded to quote Antonio Rosmini (*La perfezione cristiana, Pagine di ascetica*):

> Reflect on this thought, that sanctity consists in being willing to be opposed and humiliated, rightly or wrongly; in being willing to obey; in being willing to wait, with perfect serenity; in doing the will of your superiors without regard for your own will; in acknowledging all the benefits you receive and your own unworthiness; in feeling a great gratitude to others, and especially to God's ministers; in sincere love; in tranquillity, resignation, gentleness, and the desire to do good to all, and in unceasing work. I am about to leave and can say no more, but this is enough.

This is enough, fully enough, to describe the pattern of every apostle and of every saint in the pattern of an apostle. This is also enough to give a perfect reversal of the stratagems and devices by which Satan has brought his rebellion into human history and has beguiled the human race into sorrow.

No one can masquerade better as Christ than the Wounder of the World, and he has had many disguises in this age. But there is a sure difference; the one who wounds will not permit himself to be wounded. To accept wounds is not the manner of disobedience. But it is very much the way of perfect freedom: "The Son of Man must suffer many things" (Mt 8:31). "I must be about my Father's business" (Lk 2:49). "I must preach the Kingdom" (Lk 4:43). "I must abide at your house" (Lk 19:5). "The Son of Man must be delivered into the hands of sinful men" (Lk 24:7). "The Son of Man must be lifted up" (Jn 5:14). "I must do the work of him who sent me" (Jn 9:4).

Independence is an occasion for freedom, but it is not *the* freedom (cf. Gal 5:13). Independence is a chance to choose the good, but real freedom is the choice. We are independent "of" but we are free "for". Independence is declared; freedom is accepted. Independence, like Bartholdi's statue looking for an honest land and Diogenes looking for an honest man, holds a lamp to light the way; freedom is the lamp itself like John the Baptist, and the light of the lamp like Jesus Christ (cf. Jn 5:33; 8:12). The human will is capable of independence; but it accomplishes freedom only when it ceases to "put darkness for light and light for darkness".

Born Free

Consequently, freedom requires conformity to the structure of Christ's Body as it is made visible in the hierarchical constitution of the Church. This structure is not a bureaucracy; it is an organism for sacrifice. Disobedience to the hierarchical nature of the Church, for instance, does not eliminate the priests; it eliminates the sacrifice they offer. It does a double disservice, for it tends to laicize the priest, which is completely erroneous; and it lets loose an archaic kind of clericalism, such as we see in the various abuses of privilege, an example being the unwarranted proliferation of extraordinary ministers of the Eucharist. It is a distraction from the proper order of service to God which is perfect freedom. The clericalist says with the chief captain: "With a great sum obtained I this freedom." The sacerdotalist says with St. Paul: "But I was born free" (Acts 22:28).

A second form of obedience is to a ritual consciousness. Mary is the model of worship, and in every Marian mystery — Sorrowful, Joyful, and Glorious — there is a sense of occasion. But the egoist, in private captivity to disobedience, does not want such elegant freedom. Pope Leo XIII located the tendency in American culture. He admired the characteristic American virtues of fortitude and industry. He told America's first saint: "We must work, Cabrini, we must work. We have eternity to rest." But he also knew the limits of work without eternity. For a little example of the way American ingenuity in the natural virtues contrasts with our awkwardness in living the supernatural virtues, consider that astonishing invention, the Electric Imitation Church Candle. We have discovered a way to offer a sacrifice and keep it, too. What does it signify? To offer God an electric candle is like Abraham sacrificing Isaac in a microwave oven. This is a banality which, like weak syntax and poor diction in the liturgy, indicates a disintegrating sense of self-offering without which the personality is not integral.

There is a reason why the priest properly does not wear flimsy vestments. Every priestly stole, each chasuble, has two thousand years of weight in its threads. The High Priest entered the Holy of Holies laden with symbols of the twelve tribes; the priest of Christ carries the whole of mankind to lead them in the *Sanctus*. The priestly soul has two thousand years and more of great grace to bear that weight, if only the grace and the weight are accepted together. Some church supply catalogues advertise that their tawdry vestments are "cheap and light-weight". The priest would be that, too, if he bought them for that.

Because Atlas in myth was not a priest, the world on his back became a cross; because Christ in fact is a priest, the cross on his back becomes the world. But the modern person, bereft of the priestly sense, finds burdens intolerable. He says what no other age said so much: there are too many people for comfort and too few people for company, too many pressures and not enough challenges, too many commitments and little worth commitment, too many distractions and not much that is attractive, an abundance of poverty and a superabundance of wealth, too much time on our hands and too little time in our lives; he says the world is growing unbearable for the curious reason that it is growing smaller every day. If it is small enough to fit on human shoulders it will certainly be unsupportable; if it is large enough to be shouldered by all the ages and a succession of all the apostles, then it will support the human shoulders. This is, if you will, the priestly principle of inter-cession; the priestly soul does not endure alone, it perdures with Christ. And thus the Pope is Vicar of Christ and not a Vicar of Atlas. As our Holy Father closed the jubilee doors of the Holy Year, he wore an embroidered cope which looked as though it would crush a lesser man: "Take my yoke upon you and learn of me." Predictably, there will continue to be some who have breathed in so much air of secularity that their lungs cannot sustain a ritual burden. We have to be cautious with such people. The secular experience has shown that anyone who removes the yoke from his own shoulders places it on someone else.

A girl about four years old ran her fingers over the life-sized Pietà in her suburban parish and asked her own mother, "Why does Jesus have boo-boos?" It was a child's question and therefore not childish. Gregory of Nazianzus asked it; so did Hilary of Poitiers and Abelard. The prophet Zechariah asked: "What are these wounds in your hands?" And the answer came back, "Those with which I was wounded in the house of my friends" (Zech 13:6). But the disordered mentality wants only independence and so it flees wounds, which in the divine economy means fleeing from Christ. Eventually, it makes mere independence a prison house of the intellect and will. This at least in part explains the meretriciousness of much commentary about freedom and obedience in the last generation. At the fourth assembly of the Synod of Bishops in 1977, the future Pope John Paul I, Albino Luciani, remarked:

> Catechists and theologians are often bound together by a mass of publications which are at times neither controlled nor read and assimilated critically. Bishops are to exercise greater vigilance and make use of the theologians themselves. They are to recognize the particular charism of theologians which however is usefully explicated only if placed humbly at the service of the Bishops in full respect for the Magisterium, without trying to constitute a Church of professors opposed to the Shepherd, or which conditions them through pressure groups linked with the publishing industry, universities, and theological associations.

Pride blinds the soul to such common sense. In the pathology of Judas, who set himself up as a censor of the bishop of his soul, are the four stages in the spiritual degeneration caused by independence as an end in itself; each is a symptom of the modern spiritual decay. The first stage is irreverence: Judas objects to the use of precious ointment on Christ instead of its expenditure on social services, as if they were contradictory.

The second stage is sentimentalism: Judas decides to manipulate with a kiss the one he had betrayed. His pale touch in
moonlight is a calculated substitute for sacrificial love, a cruel
sensitivity session. Sentimentalism sacrifices everything for love
except itself. The third stage is distrust. In his cynicism, Judas
will not confess his sins, so he spurns the solution and repents
in his own hollowness. And the fourth stage is disobedience;
having concluded that he had grown more prudent than God,
and then discovering that the experience of God outlives the
senility of the world, Judas takes his life instead of giving it.

The story of redemption has not ended that way. It is better
to remember what the power of holy obedience did to Peter.
He was a sinner but he was not a cynic. He thought himself an
independent man the night he denied Christ, but on Easter he
found himself in a freer world; as such, he represents consciousness in transition beyond modernity. There is no finer testimony to the liberating Christ than the First Letter of Peter.

Independent Peter marveled to find a coin in the mouth of a
fish. Free Peter writes: "It was not with perishable things such
as gold and silver that you are redeemed" (1 Pet 1:18).

Independent Peter once was called Satan. Free Peter writes:
"Brethren, be sober and vigilant for your adversary the Devil
roams like a roaring lion seeking whom he may devour" (1 Pet
4:7).

Independent Peter fell asleep as his Master prayed. Free Peter
writes: "The end of all things is near, therefore be clearminded
and self-controlled so that you can pray" (1 Pet 4:7).

Independent Peter's voice choked: "I never knew the man."
Free Peter writes: "Always be prepared to give an answer to
everyone who asks you to give the reason for the hope you
have" (1 Pet 3:15).

Independent Peter was asked, "Do you love me? Feed my
sheep." Free Peter writes: "Be shepherds of God's flock that is

under your care, not because you must, but because you are willing, as God wants you to be. . . . And when the chief shepherd appears, you will receive a crown of glory that will never fade away" (1 Pet 5:4).